PENGUIN BOOKS
THE BOOK OF AVATARS AND DIVINITIES

Bulbul Sharma is the author of five collections of short stories, a novel, three books for children and a work of non-fiction. Her books have been translated into several languages. She divides her time between New Delhi and Goa.

Namita Gokhale is the author of sixteen works of fiction and non-fiction, including the cult classic *Paro: Dreams of Passion*. Gokhale has also written the Puffin Mahabharata and *Lost in Time: Ghatotkacha and the Game of Illusions*. Her edited anthologies include *Himalaya: Adventures, Meditations, Life* and *The Himalayan Arc: Journeys East of South-east*. Gokhale is the founder and co-director of the Jaipur Literature Festival and of Mountain Echoes, the Bhutan Literature Festival. She is the director of Yatra Books.

Nanditha Krishna has a PhD in ancient Indian culture from the University of Bombay. She has been a professor and research guide for the PhD programme of C.P.R. Institute of Indological Research, affiliated to the University of Madras. She was the honorary director and later president of the C.P. Ramaswami Aiyar Foundation, and is the founder-director of its constituents, including the Kanchi Museum of Folk Art. She is the author of several notable books, including *Sacred Plants of India, Sacred Animals of India, Hinduism and Nature, Madras Then, Chennai Now* and *The Arts and Crafts of Tamilnadu*.

Parvez Dewan is an officer of the Indian Administrative Service. His previous books include *The Hanuman Chalisa of Goswami Tulasi Das, The Names of Allah* and *Jammu-Kashmir-Ladakh: Travel, Trekking, Art, Culture and Society.*

Royina Grewal has written two monographs on Chanderi and Mandu as well as *Sacred Virgin: Travels along the Narmada, In Rajasthan: A Travelogue* and *In the Shadow of the Taj*. Her interest in history is expressed in the six son et lumière productions she has conceived, scripted and directed. Grewal and her husband divide their time between Delhi and an organic farm in Rajasthan.

Seema Mohanty is a freelance writer based in Mumbai. She wrote *The Book of Kali* based on the lectures and writings of her brother, Devdutt Pattanaik, the well-known mythologist.

THE BOOK OF
AVATARS AND
DIVINITIES

Introduction by Nanditha Krishna

PENGUIN BOOKS

An imprint of Penguin Random House

PENGUIN BOOKS

USA | Canada | UK | Ireland | Australia
New Zealand | India | South Africa | China | Singapore

Penguin Books is part of the Penguin Random House group of companies
whose addresses can be found at global.penguinrandomhouse.com

Published by Penguin Random House India Pvt. Ltd
4th Floor, Capital Tower 1, MG Road,
Gurugram 122 002, Haryana, India

Penguin
Random House
India

First published in Penguin Books by Penguin Random House India 2018

10 9 8 7 6 5 4 3 2

ISBN 9780143446880

Typeset in Adobe Caslon Pro by Manipal Digital Systems, Manipal

Printed at Manipal Technologies Limited, India

www.penguin.co.in

MIX
Paper | Supporting
responsible forestry
FSC® C043100

This is a legitimate digitally printed version of the book and therefore might not
have certain extra finishing on the cover.

Contents

Introduction

It is often said that Hindus worship thirty-three million gods. I don't know who invented that number, but it is as mythical as the stories surrounding the gods of Hinduism. There are several deities and divinities who are a part of the history of Hinduism, each with an elaborate literature establishing his or her divinity.

Hindus believe in one Supreme Being or Brahman who is nirguna or without qualities, with neither a physical appearance nor physical attributes. But the devotee may conceive the Supreme Being as he wills, which is generally saguna or with attributes. The Saguna Brahman may be a personal god or an incarnation, a natural phenomenon (like a mountain or river) or even a form of zoolatry. Many deities represent important historical or environmental events or the social evolution from grazing to food production. Each deity has a complex and distinct personality. From the myriad deities of the Hindu pantheon, a devotee chooses to worship the divinity most suited to his or her disposition. Some deities like Vishnu, Shiva and Shakti have their own individual cults and followers; others are a part of a complex tradition of multiple deities who lead the path to a Nirguna Brahman.

The Supreme Being or Nirguna Brahman of Hinduism is very different from the one god of the Abrahamic religions. If Jehovah or Allah is a mighty ruler sitting in his kingdom of heaven in the sky, with the power to pardon the sinner or reward his devotee, Brahman is found everywhere, within us and without, irrespective of whether you are a worshipper or not, in humans and even animals. The Abrahamic god is far removed from his human followers, for they are monotheistic religions that separate god and people. In contrast, Hinduism is a monistic religion where, in spite of the multiplicity of deities, there is an awareness that they are all part of one Supreme Being, as are human beings and animals. There is no distinction or duality between mind and matter, or god and the world. The individual divinities are but a manifestation of the genderless Brahman, who is the Ultimate Reality.

Hindu divinities have evolved over millennia, with new ones appearing over the years and many forgotten as the forms of worship changed. They evolved from thirty-three Vedic devas or 'shining ones' who represent the forces of nature and the moral values of the times. Thus Indra was the rain, Varuna the waters and Agni the fire. Vishnu was the all-pervading sun, along with Surya and Savitr, while Ushas was the dawn. Pushan represented agriculture. Dyauspitr was the father of the shining ones and Prithvi was Mother Earth. The rivers—especially the mighty Saraswati—were sacred, for they gave water for sustenance. The Vedic people depended on a capricious nature for their survival and established the concept of sacred nature. Five thousand years ago, the sages of the

Rig Veda showed a clear appreciation of the natural world and its ecology. Asuras were initially 'leaders' among the Vedic people. Towards the end of the Rig Veda, it is said that they were banished to the north and became synonymous with demons. The gods, or devas, represent light and are constantly battling the demons, or asuras, who represent the forces of darkness. If the devas and asuras represent the opposing forces of light and darkness, it is also a battle between the human ego and the alter ego. The deva–asura dichotomy represents the inner battles within the self.

In the epic and puranic periods, the situation changes. The devas represent goodness, and the asuras evil. Vishnu, Shiva and Devi become all-powerful, each with an entire literature of his or her own. Later, Brahma, Vishnu and Shiva combine to form a trinity of the Creator, Preserver and Destroyer. Brahma's consort is Saraswati, the goddess of learning, while Vishnu's consort is Lakshmi, or Shridevi (prosperity) and Bhudevi (earth). Shiva's consort has complex manifestations such as Parvati, the gentle daughter of the Himalayas, Sati, who threw herself into the fire to avenge her husband, and Durga or Shakti, the source of all energy. But the gods also combine to form Harihara and Shankara-Narayana (Vishnu-Shiva) or the androgynous Ardhanarishwara, a combination of Shiva and Parvati. Each god is given attributes and weapons and an animal vahana or vehicle: Shiva's primary attribute is the trident or trishul and his vehicle is the bull; Vishnu's primary attributes include the conch and discus, while his vehicle is Garuda the eagle; Brahma holds a kamandalu (pot of water), rosary beads and palm leaves befitting a rishi, and his vehicle is the swan. Similarly, Lakshmi may be identified by her lotus seat and elephants, Durga by her lion vehicle and Saraswati by her veena and swan vehicle. In time, a rich iconography and several myths developed not only for the main deities themselves but for their many manifestations and incarnations which became a part of the great tapestry of Hindu theism.

Different myths associated with the gods represent natural or social phenomena. For example, the battle between Indra and Vritra in the Rig Veda represents the destruction of drought (Vritra) by rain (Indra). Similarly, the battle between goddess Durga and the buffalo deity Mahisha represents the war between the food producers who worshipped the goddess and the pastoralists who grazed buffaloes.

A Hindu icon—murti, pratima or vigraha—may be an image made of stone, metal, terracotta or even a painting, but it is never regarded as the Supreme Being himself. The image represents an association of ideas that are of value to the devotee. When an icon or idol is worshipped, it is regarded as the spirit of the deity and a point of concentration for the worshipper, yet the idea of Brahman or the Supreme Reality is never confined within it. The gods are superhuman manifestations of their worshippers. If humans have two hands, gods have many, representing their many superior abilities. The four-faced Brahma represents the height of wisdom, for he has more brainpower than an ordinary person.

By the eighth century, there were so many 'cults' that Adi Shankara, a great saint of that period, established six primary cults that made up Sanatana Dharma, or the Eternal Religion—Shaiva, Vaishnava, Saurya, Kaumara, Ganapatya and Shakta, associated with Shiva, Vishnu, Surya, Kumara (or Kartikeya), Ganapati and Shakti— giving him the title of *shanmata sthapana acharya* (the teacher who established the six cults). Initially, Hindu deities and their various forms were supposed to be within these six cults that Adi Shankara recognized but, in time, many more deities were gradually absorbed by the ever-expanding Hindu religion such that today the number of deities far exceeds the original number envisaged by Adi Shankara. These six cults are not to be confused with the six schools of philosophy—*yoga*, *vaisheshika*, *vedanta*, *nyaya*, *samkhya* and *mimamsa*. The religion was called Sanatana Dharma, the eternal law of righteousness, which had to triumph above all else.

Hindu divinities are treated with the love and care that would be given to a beloved parent or child. In temples, they are woken up to prayer, bathed, dressed, fed (with naivedya or food offerings) and invoked with music and dance. The ritual is called puja, which is a devotional activity in a temple, home or within one's heart. There are no rules, no insistence on daily or weekly prayers or a visit to the temple. Moksha or the liberation of the soul is the goal of every individual and the effort has to be one's own.

From time to time the gods appear on earth. Vishnu is one of the trinity of Brahma (preserver), Shiva (destroyer) and Vishnu (preserver). To destroy the forces of evil and safeguard good, Vishnu incarnates on earth from time to time. The concept of an avatar (incarnation) developed quite early in Hinduism. An avatar is a deity descended on earth, loosely called an incarnation, but actually translated as 'descent' or 'appearance'. An avatar may be partial like the first six incarnations of Vishnu, or whole like Rama and Krishna. While the various forms of each deity are manifestations, the concept of avatar is generally associated with Vishnu. The origin of this concept goes back to the Rig Veda, where Indra is endowed with the power to assume any form he desires. As Indra's friend and associate, Vishnu inherits this ability in the form of the avatar which he assumes to save the earth and destroy evil.

In the Bhagavad Gita (IV.7–8) Krishna says,

Yadā yadā hi dharmasya glānir bhavati bhārata
Abhyutthānam adharmasya tadātmānam srijāmyaham
Paritrānāya sādhūnām vināśāya ca dushkritām
Dharma samsthāpanārthāya sambhavāmi yuge yuge

which means

Whenever there is a decline of righteousness, O descendant of Bharata, and a rise of unrighteousness, then I manifest myself.

To protect the pious, to destroy the wicked, and to re-establish righteousness, I am reborn, in every age.

As I have detailed in the section on Vishnu, his avatars are generally ten: Matsya (fish), Kurma (tortoise), Varaha (boar), Narasimha (man-lion), Vamana (dwarf), Parashurama (Rama with the axe), Rama (the perfect man), Krishna (the total incarnation), Buddha (the man of wisdom) and Kalki (a future incarnation). The number fluctuates, from eleven in the Vishnu Purana to twenty-two in the Bhagavata Purana.

Who are the avatars? Some represent the story of environmental events. For example, Matsya the fish, the first incarnation of Vishnu, represents a great flood of the past, maybe the great deluge which submerged Dwaraka, Krishna's capital, where the only temple dedicated to Matsya is found. In Vamana we see the sun's inexorable suppression of the produce of the land, whose harvest is still celebrated annually as Onam in Kerala. Varaha the boar, who pulls up roots and shoots, taught man to plough the land.

Some of the avatars were local tribal deities who were absorbed into Hinduism. Kurma is the story of the tortoise, the god of the Bhil tribes. Narasimha the man-lion was the deity of the Chenchu tribes of Andhra Pradesh who live in the region around Ahobilam, where the cave temples of Narasimha are found atop a hill.

And then there are the great figures who are part of pre- and proto-historic times. Parashurama represents the battle between the Brahmins and Kshatriyas for supremacy. Rama is the perfect man, the king of Ayodhya whose kingdom or Rama Rajya was the ideal land and model for future rulers. His story is immortalized in the epic Ramayana. Krishna is divinity for Hindus, who incarnated to free the land from injustice. His story is immortalized in the epic Mahabharata. Buddha, a figure from ancient history, is the man of peace and Kalki the avatar of the future.

If Vishnu incarnates, Shiva manifests several times. It may be an anugraha (kind, blessing) form such as Pashupati, the lord of animals. It may be an angry samhara (destructive) murti, a ferocious destroyer of evil. In this form he is Rudra, Ugra, Kalantaka, Gajantaka, Tripurantaka and Kamantaka who destroyed the evil Gajasura, Tripura and even Kama the Indian Cupid who broke his meditation. As Nataraja, the lord of dance, he represents the continuous process of creation, preservation and destruction. But the lord of dance is also a silent spiritual yogi who meditates as Dakshinamurti. He may appear in his aniconic form, the Linga, and burst out of it as Lingodbhava. And he combines with Vishnu to become Hari-Hara or Shankara-Narayana and with Devi to become Ardhanarishvara. The section on Shiva in this book, written by Namita Gokhale, begins with an evocation of his 108 names and acquaints the reader with the myths, symbolism and the different traditions that have evolved around him.

There are probably more forms of Devi than any other deity, for temples are dedicated to the goddess in every Indian village. She is energy and power, the ultimate destroyer of evil. She may be Shakti, Durga, Lakshmi, Saraswati, or she may be a local village goddess with an unknown name, but all-powerful and commanding. The worship of the goddess is probably the most ancient form of worship in India. During the festival of Navaratri or Dussehra, she is worshipped for ten days, when she fought and killed the powerful Mahisha, the buffalo-god of the pastoral tribes of ancient India, who were gradually pushed into the deep forest by the agriculturists. The section on Devi in this book, written by Bulbul Sharma, begins with a verse from the *Devimahatmyam* and recounts the many myths and legends associated with her various forms.

The chapter on the enigmatic Kali within the Devi section has been written by Seema Mohanty and the illustration is by Devdutt Pattanaik. Kali is a goddess whose worship is widespread and found all over India. The most famous Kali temple is in Kolkata whose original name was Kali ghat. Kali is identified with Durga in Sanskrit literature. She is most often a village goddess who is propitiated with sacrificial offerings of blood and wine. She is worshipped out of fear rather than love and devotion. As she is a goddess of battlegrounds and cremation grounds, her temples are generally situated outside the village. Kali worship is associated with Tantrism and sexual acts too are part of Tantrik rites to invoke Kali.

Hinduism regards animals as equal to humans. Apart from the avatars, this is manifest in two popular deities—Ganesha and Hanuman. Ganesha is the elephant-headed son of Shiva and Parvati, without whom no ritual may begin and who ensures the success of every endeavour by removing obstacles from one's path, not unlike the elephant who clears the forest pathways of obstacles. The section on Ganesha, written by Royina Grewal, includes the different stories of how Ganesha acquired his form and what it represents.

Hanuman, the Vanara, is the faithful devotee of Rama, whose loyalty to Rama and devotion to the path of righteousness have sanctified him. The section on Hanuman, written by Parvez Dewan, reveals his different attributes and what he symbolizes. Today, these two gods are often more popular than the other gods of Hinduism.

In this book we are introduced to the divinities and avatars of Hinduism, a great variety spread out all over the country but uniting to become a single mystical power for the triumph of good over evil. The works of seven individual authors have been edited and combined by Penguin to bring together the forces of positivity, reminding us that we will always need a divine force to deliver us from the forces of negativity that are manifest in this world.

October 2018   Nanditha Krishna

GANESHA

Shree Ganeshaaya Namaha
(Salutations to you, O Ganesha)

All Hindu prayers, all new endeavours, all the simple routines of daily life and especially all new books are preceded by this invocation.

Since Ganesha is very specially the patron deity of writers and since all books exist in his mind, the invocation to the elephant-headed god used by the Chalukya king Someshvara Malla at the beginning of his work *Manasollasa* is appropriate:

> *I prostrate myself before you, O Ganeshvara,*
> *Your icon is a hallowed charm*
> *That assures fulfilment of all desire.*
> *With the fanning of your broad ears,*
> *You scatter away all obstacles,*
> *As though they were weightless as cotton.*

To call upon Ganesha at the beginning of a new book is particularly important, for as Ganesha made it possible for sage Vyasa to complete the Mahabharata, so too did he impede the sage's compilation of the Puranas when he was not invoked.

3

Ganesha is one of the most widely worshipped deities in India, regarded by millions with love and adoration. Simple everyday routines, a new business, a journey, even an examination—all are preceded by a prayer to Ganesha, beseeching his benediction. Even little children in some parts of the country begin their writing lessons with the invocation *Harih Sri Ganapataya namaha* (Salutations to Ganesha, son of Shiva).

Ganesha is many things to many people. He is the portly, merry and mischievous childlike god, as well as the abstract philosopher. To his devotees he is the creator of the universe (a role more generally ascribed to Brahma) and also Siddhidata, the one who bestows blessings. He is the lord of obstacles, who removes impediments, but also creates all manner of difficulties if not propitiated. He is the presiding deity of material riches, and also the lord of spirituality. He is the guardian of the threshold who combats evil influences. To some he is also their primary personal god, their ishtadevta. Above all, Ganesha, more than any other deity, satisfies human aspirations for worldly success and fulfilment.

Ganesha is also a most accommodating deity, easy to please. He does not demand lengthy penance or austerities of his devotees but is contented by simple devotion, provided only that it is sincere.

Symbolism

The images of Ganesha proliferated as the centuries went by and a complex iconography evolved to reflect the multiple facets of this much-loved deity. All representations of his sacred form follow the strict rules enshrined in the ancient canons of iconography, the shilpa shastras. These prescribe every detail of the depiction of a deity, in painting as well as sculpture.

In these texts, Ganesha is described as a deity with the body of a human and the head of an elephant. One of the tusks is broken. He has a rotund form with a prominent pot-belly and is red-hued. In his hands and often even his trunk, he holds various symbolic objects. When seated, one leg is folded, the other rests on a footstool, and a variety of food is spread at his feet. A mouse sits near the food looking up at the deity, as though asking his permission to partake of the repast.

This familiar iconographic form of Ganesha is not just the product of a set of norms for representation in art. It is also a powerful visual manifestation of religious belief, imbued with philosophical meaning. Complex abstract concepts are depicted through a variety of symbols and thus communicated to the devout. Iconography goes far beyond the obvious for those who seek to contemplate it deeply. Even the most minute detail of an image recalls episodes in the mythical life of the deity and leads to a deeper understanding of the sacred reality he embodies. Each detail is resonant with layers of meaning, a quality that enables Ganesha to be many things to many people.

Ganesha's body is stunted, almost childlike, and conforms to iconographic norms prescribed for a five-year-old male child. These stipulate that the head and torso be noticeably longer than the legs. The childlike aspect is reinforced by a pronounced chubbiness, which elicits an indulgent affection. It also recalls the specially close bond between Ganesha and his mother.

Ganesha is always visualized as an elephant-headed deity. There are no depictions of his form prior to his beheading or even of the episode of the beheading itself. His significance within the Hindu pantheon rests in his rebirth with an elephant head, which is always one-fifth of the body and is a symbol of his immense wisdom. It is frequently white, recalling the divine white elephant Airavata, whose head, according to one myth, was attached to Ganesha's body after his beheading. (The colour white also signifies purity and the peaceful temperament associated with Ganesha in several of his manifestations.) Images of Ganesha within or inspired by the Tantrik tradition often depict him with multiple heads, normally ranging in number from three to five.

His small but penetrating eyes are said to see the spirit of the divine in all creation and to perceive the essential unity in the diversity of the world. Usually Ganesha's eyes are red, like those of an elephant, with dark pupils, leading to his name Krishnapingaksha, the black-and-red-eyed one. While in some early sculpture the eyes are depicted very much like those of an elephant, artisans over the centuries have attempted to give them a more human dimension. The face has been flattened and the eyes positioned towards the front rather than the sides, as would have been normal for an elephant.

The eyes have also become larger, sometimes complete with eyebrows and often carefully contrived to convey a very human compassion, sometimes even a glimmer of amusement. On occasion, the eyes are placed close together, with both pupils near the inner edge, creating an angry, almost enraged, expression. This is a demonic manifestation of Ganesha that recalls his early choleric disposition, which required propitiation. Some icons present Ganesha with a third eye, like his father. The three eyes are said to represent the sun, the moon and fire.

The tilak on his forehead is in the form of Shiva's three-pronged trishul and clearly identifies him as a devotee of his father. It is also said to signify Ganesha's dominance over the three worlds—heaven, earth and the underworld—and to symbolize the three modes of being, satvik (purity), rajasik (passion) and tamasik (inertia), over which he has total control.

Ganesha is always depicted with his left tusk broken, hence his popular name Ekadanta, the single-tusked one. Many a story is told of its breaking, including one where Ganesha ends up cursing the moon to disappear. On the gods' insistence, he modifies his curse, causing the moon to wax and wane instead.

To indicate Ganesha's dominance over the moon, he is sometimes shown wearing it as an ornament in his headdress, an element that also recalls the iconography of his father Shiva.

In another story, Ganesha loses his tusk as he dutifully fulfils his role as the guardian of the entrance to his parents' chamber. He had earlier lost his head while manfully guarding the door to Parvati's bath. His role as a guardian continues to be expressed in the placement of the images above thresholds of homes as well as temples, which he shields from the ingress of evil influences. This placement also ensures that worshippers address the elephant-headed deity before entering, thus obtaining his benediction and the assurance of success.

The broken tusk is often held in one of Ganesha's hands and is considered to represent the ascetic's staff, the yoga danda, given to him by Shiva. It reinforces the ascetic aspect of Ganesha's persona, a manifestation associated with his father, the greatest of all yogis. On occasion, the tusk is also held in one of his hands as a writing instrument, recalling Ganesha's status as the god of learning.

The single tusk, as opposed to the more usual pair, is also said to remind the devout that the deity has transcended the limitation of opposites—such as the self and other, likes and dislikes, good and bad—that hold mankind in their thrall. He is dwandwa-ateetha, beyond dualities, attached to neither.

The story of Ganesha's fall from his mouse is also associated with another element of his iconography. For after his fall, the deity picked up the reptile and tied it around his distended belly—which is why he is always depicted with a snake around his midriff, or draped across his torso in replication of the sacred thread that indicates his sacred status. Anthropologists are tempted to see the incorporation of the snake in the iconography of Ganesha as a symbol that commemorates the victory of a tribe with an elephant totem over one that worshipped the snake. Since the snake is also an emblem of fertility, it emphasizes Ganesha's prestige as the lord of prosperity—a connotation further enhanced by the Nagas that are often sculpted in friezes in close proximity to icons of Ganesha. These reptiles are also associated with Shiva, and thus signify the bond of shared power between father and son.

According to another interpretation, the snake represents the kundalini, the cosmic energy coiled at the base of the spine. This rises when stimulated by yoga, through seven chakras, or energy centres, to the last one, at the crown of the head, where it merges with the Infinite. Ganesha is muladhara adhipati, lord of the muladhara or root chakra, the first of the seven chakras, through which the kundalini must rise, and therefore presides over the beginning of the process of release.

Many a philosophical message is drawn from Ganesha's elephantine anatomy. His trunk, for example, is said to be an embodiment of his viveka, or prudence. Just as elephants use their trunks to discriminate between succulent morsels and unpalatable foods, so too is Ganesha able to distinguish between reality and illusion. Other analogies compare the elephant's ability to uproot a tree as well as pick up a needle from the ground with its trunk to Ganesha's ability to penetrate the realms of the material as well as the transcendental—an objective towards which human-kind must aspire.

The positioning of the trunk is of considerable significance. In most representations of the deity, it is curved to the left, the side of the body associated with the ida naadi, one of the conduits of the subtle body, associated with the moon. When the trunk is placed to the right, the deity, then called Siddhi Vinayaka, requires very special and carefully structured worship. This is because the pingalaa naadi on the right of the body is associated with the sun and is said to cause destruction if the rules of worship are violated. Images with the trunk straight down are considered rare and special as this posture signifies that the sushumna, the energy channel that runs through the spine past the six chakras, is entirely open—a situation that indicates the easy movement of the kundalini and is a stage aspired to by all yogis. But most special of all are images with the trunk swung right up in the air. This position indicates that the kundalini has reached the sahasra chakra at the crown of the head, signifying the attainment of moksha.

Ganesha's big elephant ears flapping gently symbolize the winnowing away of obstacles. While their movement is also perceived to brush away negativity, their size testifies to his capacity to listen to the eternal truths of Vedanta. His large head denotes his proficiency in reflecting upon these truths and also recalls his supreme wisdom.

Although Ganesha is usually depicted with four arms, some images have as many as fourteen or even eighteen. To the primitive mind multiple arms represented supernatural powers and the ability to do many things at the same time. The more philosophical see his four arms as symbols of the four qualities of the mind—manasa (intellect), buddhi (wisdom), ahamkara (ego) and chitta (consciousness). Ganesha himself represents the pure consciousness, the atma, that enables these four aspects to function in harmony. The four arms are also said to stand for the four directions and reinforce the belief that Ganesha controls the world.

In his four hands the elephant-headed deity holds objects, often interchanged, that identify his attributes. These symbols form a kind of visual shorthand easily understood by his devotees. They have allegorical meanings which communicate the essence of the deity. The noose and the elephant goad, the pasa and the ankusha, actually pertain to elephant trainers. Used to capture wild elephants, the noose is believed by the devout to arrest delusion, curb the ego and restrain passion. It also draws the devotee from worldly entanglements and binds him to the enduring bliss of the inner self. The goad, too, symbolizes Ganesha's role in prodding his devotees out of their inertia, in urging them on to spiritual quests. According to some, the axe represents the destruction of desire and attachment, while others view it as a symbol of the cutting away of illusion and false reasoning. The sweet modakas represent the rewards of spiritual seeking, while the lotus is synonymous with purity. It also endorses Ganesha's stature as lord of fertility and prosperity.

The modaka and the lotus, usually held in the two lower hands, are sometimes replaced by stylized hand gestures or mudras—the abhaya mudra indicating reassurance and the vara mudra which communicates the deity's blessings. Ganesha is also sometimes depicted holding objects such as the mace and discus. Usually associated with Vishnu, these reflect Vaishnavaite attempts to claim the popular elephant-headed deity as their own.

Ganesha as a child is also depicted with four arms, in which he holds a mango, a banana, a jackfruit and a stick of sugar cane, all favoured by both children and elephants.

In his trunk he often grasps a wood apple, fruit of the bel tree, sacred to Shiva. In these representation, Ganesha is depicted as a cherubic and engaging child.

Even the adult Ganesha has childlike qualities, such as his inability to resist sweets. This, as well as his very human enjoyment of the good things in life, enhances his mass appeal.

A delightful story describes Ganesha as a little boy, gorging on sweets and modakas. His tummy grew larger and larger. So much so that when he bent down to touch his parents' feet, he found that he could not perform the obeisance, because his stomach was in the way.

But there is more to Ganesha's belly than meets the eye. It indicates prosperity, with which he is closely identified. At a metaphysical level Ganesha's pot belly is said to result from his kundalini shakti which has risen up through the power of his yoga to enlarge his belly. Philosophical interpretations view Ganesha's distinctive stomach as a symbol of his ability to digest all experience and conquer all desire.

The Many Manifestations

Ganesha is worshipped in many different manifestations. According to the Ganesha Purana, the deity assumed fifty-six forms while battling the king Durasada. These differed according to the number of heads and the animals used as the deity's vahanas. Icons of each of these forms were installed in seven enclosures around the temple of Ganesha Dhundiraja at Kashi to protect the city. Even today the worship of these fifty-six forms is advocated and pilgrimages are performed on the fourth day of the suklapaksha, the bright half of the lunar month, especially on the fourteenth day of the suklapaksha of the month Magha.

Among the more important forms of Ganesha is Mahaganapati, the most important deity of the Ganapatayas, who regard this manifestation as the supreme being. Mahaganapati continues to be a popular icon, worshipped by a broad spectrum of devotees and is widely represented in art. This form of Ganesha has ten hands, each holding objects bestowed by ten deities. Among these is the fruit of the citron tree, associated with Shiva, the numerous seeds of which represent creative power. Then there is the sugar cane bow, a gift from Kama, god of love, with an arrow made of a rice shoot which was gifted by the earth. Both connote agricultural fertility. Mahaganapati also holds Varaha's mace and Vishnu's discus. A pot of jewels held in his trunk, Kubera's gift, indicates wealth and the abundance of the good things of life that the deity showers upon his devotees. A consort holds a lotus, emblem of purity, in one hand and embraces the deity with the other, while gods and demons stand in attendance. These elements represent Mahaganapati's ability to perform the functions of all the gods and his supreme dominance over them all.

Another manifestation, particularly popular in Nepal, is Heramba, protector of the weak. This form of Ganesha has five heads, the colours of which closely parallel the five aspects of Shiva—Ishana, Tatpurusha, Aghora, Vamadeva and Sadyojata—and seem to indicate Heramba's might. Heramba is astride a lion borrowed from his mother, representing royalty and ferocity. One of his ten arms caresses his consort who is seated in his lap. In representations of Ucchista Ganapati, a deity of vama marg, the left-handed path of tantra, the consort is frequently depicted nude. Worship of this manifestation is performed when the supplicant is in a ritually impure or ucchista state, that is, either naked or with remnants of food in the mouth at the time of worship.

Ganapatayas worship Ganesha in conjunction with his consort, for she is his shakti, his creative energy, through and with whom he is able to function. Her presence is also believed to recall the male and the female instincts present within each human being, which must come together to stimulate a powerful creativity.

Still other forms, most usually associated with tantra, include Haridra Ganapati, Navaneeta Ganapati, Swarna Ganapati and Samtana Ganapati. Each is worshipped with special mantras, as well as very specific yantras. These are used in complex rituals, many conducted to seek and receive material boons, especially those associated with sexuality. These forms as well as those of Mahaganapati, Heramba and Ucchista Ganapati were also associated with the six fearful abhichara rites, whereby a victim can be manipulated to experience an obsessive attraction, be completely subjugated, consumed with jealousy, immobilized, deluded or even killed.

Ganesha in Worship

An icon of Ganesha presides over the entrances to most temples dedicated to other important Hindu deities. He is also usually present in a niche at the beginning of the inner circumambulatory path, where he may be invoked even before the commencement of the initial parikrama. In Shiva temples, there is often a separate shrine to Ganesha in the south-west corner, to protect the temple from the demons that reside in that direction. Since he is also integral to the iconography of Shiva, images of Ganesha are an inherent part of temple friezes that portray episodes from the life of the great god. Even bronze statues of Shiva usually incorporate a small figurine of Ganesha—an association that endorses both Ganesha's paternity and his status as the leader of Shiva's attendants.

Ganesha is held in special reverence in Maharashtra, where eight shrines in the vicinity of Pune, collectively called the Ashta Vinayaka, attract huge numbers of worshippers. In a mythological distant past, Ganesha moved over the land, combating evil, spreading good, leaving evidence of his passage in the eight temples, each of which holds part of the sacred spiritual substance, the life force of the deity.

The Ranjangaoncha Mahaganapati temple at Ranjangaon, about 50 kilometres from Pune, enshrines the image of Mahaganapati, who is believed to have here helped Shiva destroy the citadels of the demon Tripurasura. The common myth is presented with a slightly different slant.

The demon, as many demons do, propitiated Shiva and procured from him a boon of invincibility. Girded by the powers bestowed upon him by the great god, he went on to build three great and completely impregnable citadels, for which he was called Tripurasura. Secure in his strongholds, the demon established his terrifying and despotic rule over gods and men. The gods appealed to Shiva for redress but since he had granted the boon, he was unable to help. Narada muni heard of Shiva's dilemma and advised him to address Mahaganapati, the most powerful of the gods. Shiva invoked his son with great humility and implored him to intervene. All the gods added their pleas and bestowed their weapons upon Mahaganapati, to aid him in his destruction of Tripurasura. Resplendent in his might, utterly confident and supremely powerful, Mahaganapati loosened a mighty arrow. It sang through the air, pierced each of the three impenetrable citadels of the demon and killed him instantly. And gods and men rejoiced.

A variation from South India gives us a somewhat different version in which Shiva himself fights the demon.

Moved by the distress of the inhabitants of the three worlds, Shiva set out to battle the demon. But he forgot to first seek the blessings of his son. Insulted, Mahaganapati caused the axle of Shiva's chariot to break. As Shiva fell in an undignified heap upon the ground, he became aware of his omission. He paid obeisance to his son, who then empowered his father to vanquish the demon.

Ganesha as Varadavinayaka, the bestower of boons, draws thousands of devotees at the Varadavinayaka temple near Mahad.

Thevoor, near Pune, enshrines Ganesha as Chintamani Vinayaka and is associated with the familiar myth regarding the dispute over the possession of the wish-fulfilling gem.

Gana, the son of King Abhijit and Queen Gunavati, was a great devotee of Shiva. Pleased with his homage, Shiva granted him certain powers, which unfortunately went to Gana's head and inflated his ego.

Once during a visit to sage Kapila's ashram, Gana saw Kapila's wish-fulfilling gem, Chintamani, which had been gifted to him by Shiva. He witnessed its miraculous powers and felt they were wasted on a mere sage. Gana believed he would make far better use of the Chintamani and therefore deserved to possess the jewel, When Kapila refused to give it to him, Gana summoned his army to take the gem by force. But when he reached Kapila's ashram, he found Ganesha at the head of a huge army. In the battle that followed, Gana was killed by Ganesha who then restored the Chintamani to Kapila.

The sage returned it to Ganesha. For, he said, wealth and the desire for riches are the root of many troubles of the world. He, however, implored Ganesha to reside at Thevoor forever, which the devout believe he indeed does, to this day.

At the Girijaatmaja Vinayaka temple at Lenayadri, between Pune and Nasik, Ganesha is revered as an infant.

The Ballaleshwar Vinayak temple at Pali commemorates a legend which describes how Ganapati is said to have come to the aid of a young boy, Ballal.

The powerful image is said to be Swayambhu (self-generated), and has its trunk turned to the right.

Although this position is considered special and most rare, the icon of Siddhi Vinayak at the Siddhatek temple also has the trunk to curving to the right instead of the more usual orientation towards the left. The temple is said to be located at the very site where Ganesha bestowed upon Vishnu the siddhi, the supra-normal ability, to defeat powerful demons.

The temple on top of a hill was constructed by Maharani Ahilyabai Holkar. Other temples to this aspect of Ganesha include the famous Siddhi Vinayak temple in Mumbai, as well as at Pillayarpatti in Tamil Nadu.

For his followers, Ganesha provides an anchor in a confusing, ever-changing world. He is the accessible god, compassionate and easy to please, who satisfies every human need, be it spiritual, emotional or material.

The many myths and legends about Ganesha have inspired and comforted countless millions and offered clues to the meaning and purpose of life. They are as relevant today as they ever were. It is for us to draw upon the stories and make innovations in our own lives, to renew the art of joy and love, to conquer our own demons, to see that obstacles are often self-created. Only then will Ganesha endure, releasing his life-sustaining power for all eternity.

SHIVA

Shiva has 1008 names which describe his attributes. Chanting these guarantees his grace. The scope, diversity and contrary polarities which lie behind the meanings of these names evoke the truly unknowable nature of Shiva. Let us begin with an evocation of 108 of these names.

Achaleshvar: immovable lord, the resolute one; **Adi-Nath:** primeval master; **Aghora:** non-terrifying, pleasing; **Aja:** unmanifest; **Aja-Ekapada:** one-footed lord; **Ajagandhi:** he who smells like a goat; **Akrura:** kind god; **Andhakehsvar:** dispeller of darkness; **Antak:** the ender; **Apamnidhi:** lord of the waters (semen); **Ardhanari:** half woman; **Ashani:** thunderbolt; **Asutosh:** easily pleased; **Avadhut:** naked ascetic; **Baleshvar:** long-haired; strong; **Basava:** bull; **Bhairava:** quick-tempered god; **Bhasmeshvar:** smeared with ash; **Bhava:** existence; **Bhikshatan:** celestial beggar; **Bhima:** strong one; **Bhisma:** terrible one; **Bhola:** simpleton, guileless god; **Bhootpati:** god of ghosts; **Bhuteshvara:** lord of elements; **Bhuvanesh:** lord of the world; **Bilva-Dandin:** bearer of a staff of belva; **Chandrachuda:** moon-crested; **Dakshineshvar:** god who faces the south; **Damarudharin:** bearer of the rattle-drum; **Ekavratya:** unorthodox sage; **Gajantaka:** killer of the elephant demon; **Gambhiresh:** austere ascetic; **Ganapati:** lord of ganas; **Gangadhar:** bearer of the river Ganga; **Ghora:** fearsome; **Girisha:** lord

21

of the hills; **Grihapati:** householder; **Guheshvar:** lord of the caves, mysterious one; **Hara:** router, seizer, ravisher; **Hiranyaretas:** lord of the golden seed; **Ishana:** lord; **Ishvara:** godhead; **Jambukeshvar:** lord of Jambudvipa i.e. India; **Jateshvar:** lord with matted hair; **Jimutavahan:** he who rides the clouds; **Jvareshvar:** lord of fevers; **Kaleshvar:** lord of time, lord of art; **Kamandaludhari:** bearer of the water-pot; **Kamanashe:** destroyer of desire; **Kapalin:** bearer of skulls; **Kapardin:** lord with a conch-shaped topknot; **Karpure-Gauranga:** white as camphor; **Kedar:** lord of the hills; **Kiraata:** tribal; **Krittivasa:** he who wears animal hide; **Lakulisha:** bearer of the staff; **Mahabaleshvar:** almighty one; **Mahadeva:** great god; **Maharishi:** great sage; **Mahesh:** great lord; **Maithuneshvar:** lord of sexual union; **Manish:** conqueror of the mind; **Marutta:** wind, storm; **Nageshvar:** lord of serpents; **Nagnavratadhari:** naked sage; **Nataraja:** lord of dance and drama; **Neelkantha:** blue-necked one; **Omkarnath:** lord of the mystical syllable 'Om'; **Pashaye:** lord of the noose; **Pashupati:** lord of the beasts; **Pavaka:** fire, lava; **Purusha:** cosmic spirit, the primeval man; **Rudra:** wild god, howler; **Sadjoyta:** eternally radiant; **Sailesh:** lord of mountains; **Samhari:** destroyer; **Sarva:** archer; **Shambhu:** benign; **Shankar:** benevolent, beneficent; **Sharabha:** dragon; **Shikhandin:** lord with a peacock plume; **Siddhartha:** one who is accomplished; **Somasundara:** beautiful as the moon; **Somnath:** lord of soma, the herb of vitality; **Sthanu:** the great pillar, that which is still; **Sundarmurti:** alluring body; **Svashva:** master of dogs; **Tamasopati:** lord of inertia, darkness, passivity; **Tejomaya:** radiant being; **Trilochan:** three-eyed; **Tripurantaka:** destroyer of the demon cities;

Trishuldhari: bearer of the trident; **Ugra:** fierce; **Umapati:** husband of Uma-Parvati; **Urdhvalinga:** aroused linga (life-force); **Vaidyanath:** lord of physicians; **Vamadev:** lord of the left-handed (Tantrik) paths; **Vibhuti-Bhushan:** he who is bedecked with ash marks; **Vinapani:** he who plays the lute; **Virabhadra:** the noble hero; **Vireshvar:** lord of martial arts; **Virupaksha:** lord with ill-formed malignant eyes; **Vishvanath:** lord of the universe; **Vrikshanath:** lord of trees; **Vrishabhanath:** tamer of bulls; **Yakshanath:** lord of yakshas, forest-spirits; **Yogesh:** lord of yoga

Let us meditate on Lord Shiva, the supreme ascetic. He wears the crescent moon on his forehead, from which flows the celestial river Ganga. The river represents the ceaseless flux of time and is the embodiment of the nurturing life force. Shiva's body is smeared with ash, and a tiger skin is girt around his loins. Of his four arms, one carries a trident, one an axe, and the other two are set in classical mudras, granting boons and removing fear.

Lord Shiva has three eyes, through which he can view the past, the present and the future. The third eye, that of higher perception, looks inwards. When its vision is directed outwards, the searing intensity of its gaze emblazons and destroys all it looks at. The three-eyed aspect of Shiva is variously referred to as Virupaksha, Triaksha, Trinayana and Trinetra.

The crescent moon rests like a diadem on Shiva's long matted hair. According to myth, Soma, the moon, was discredited by an assembly of the gods for some indiscretion and so cast into the ocean. Later, during the samudra

manthan, the churning of the ocean, Shiva resurrected
Soma by placing the moon on his brow, thereby restoring
the intuitive faculties to their rightful position.

The trident of Shiva, his trishul, represents the triad
of the creator, the preserver and the destroyer. His spear,
the pashupata, is the weapon with which he destroys the
universe at the dissolution of the yugas, the ordained time
cycles. His axe is called the parashu, which he gifted to
Parashurama. He also carries a club called the khatvanga,
which has a skull at its head. Around his neck is a garland of
skulls, which earns him the epithet of Kapalin. The drum
in his hand, the damaru, heralds the dance of creation,
just as the ashes which anoint him signify the forces of
destruction ever present in all that is living.

Shiva is accompanied in popular iconography by his
wife Parvati, a beauteous ever-auspicious figure who shares
his austerities and penance. Seated beside them is their
son Ganesha, the elephant-headed remover of obstacles,
and Skanda, or Kartika, their second son. The sacred bull
Nandi, representing the powers of fecundity, procreation
and constancy, is also a member of this divine family.

Shiva is the god of life and death, of destruction and
rebirth. The whole life process is imminent in him, but he
transcends it and inhabits a mental, emotional and spiritual
space which is difficult to understand through intellectual
processes alone. To embrace Shiva, to comprehend his
power, involves an intuitive leap into our deepest inner
selves.

The mythopoeic mind assigns attributes to godheads,
visible symbols to unrepresentable mysteries. The attributes

of a saguna, qualified god, is therefore completely different from the non-attributes of a nirguna, non-qualified god. Hindu divinity gives us an infinite variety and hierarchy of gods and goddesses to worship and aspire to, so that we may seek the version of saguna reality most suited to the accidental permutations of our personality and situation.

The Puranic tales contain a sense of timelessness. They are elastic and energetic and in a constant state of reinterpretation and reinvention. There has always been a remarkable flexibility between the oral and written traditions, and the immensely popular television mega-serials on the Hindu gods are an appropriation of technology and media by an ancient and uninterrupted culture. The Ramayana and Mahabharata television epics, aired on the national channel Doordarshan in the late 1980s and early 1990s created the conditions for the revival of both moderate and fundamental religious forces in India. While the Epic of Gilgamesh, the Odyssey, the Iliad and even the Old Testament may lose their immediate relevance to society, the Hindu sacred and religious literature reinsinuates itself back into the mainstream of life and technology with a startling contemporaneity.

India, with its infamous lack of the historical sense of time, with its non-linear approach to ideas and events, has managed to retain a sense of the dynamic and the interactive with reference to its mythology. The gods are still alive in India. They are not symbols or emblems of abstract conceptions, but vibrant anthropomorphic realities in the living faith of the river of Hinduism, flowing uninterrupted from the beginning of historically recorded time.

Lord Shiva is one aspect of the holy trinity of Brahma, Vishnu and Mahesh. Brahma is the creator and preceptor of life. Vishnu is the preserver of the divine movement of life, representing the forces of balance and equilibrium. Mahesh, another name of Shiva, is the greatest of the gods, for he alone is the god of death and resurrection, of the flux of being and non-being.

Shiva is the primeval, primordial aspect of these enduring and eternal forces. His worship is not for the weak minded, for the vision of the universe that Shiva offers us is as stark as it is magnificent. Shiva's father-in-law, Himavata, is the lord of riches and wealth, but the supreme ascetic disdains mere wealth and demands of his followers a life of awesome austerity and penances. Kubera, the god of wealth, owes allegiance to none other than the Lord Shiva, yet Shiva himself is a naked ascetic with a skull for a begging bowl.

The evolution of Shiva as both a concept and an anthropomorphic figure is a movement as natural as the flow of the river of faith. Shiva first appears in the historical consciousness in the figure of Pashupati, on the seals of Mohenjo-Daro, 2500 BC. This early iconography portrays Shiva seated in a yogic posture, in the Siddhasana, with feet crossed beneath the erect penis, the urdhva linga. The image bears three faces and with two arms. He is surrounded in this seal by representations of an elephant, a tiger, a rhinoceros and a buffalo. Similar seals of a deity holding a trident and accompanied by a bull have also been found at these sites. Over the millennia the iconic image changes, but never essentially. The accretations of myth and interpretation cannot shake this austere and enduring ascetic.

Many indigenous tribal myths have also converged and been appropriated into the mainstream of the Shiva cult. The cult of Rudra-Shiva shows distinct influences of the great Shamanic tradition of Siberia and Central Asia. This ancient Shamanistic ethos had devolved into the pre-Buddhist traditions of the ancient religion of the Bon-po, and was also concurrent with the local Shamanistic religious systems of the aboriginal tribes of India. The use of the skull and the skeleton in mystical ceremony and much of the Tantrik approach shares common antecedents with these traditions, as demonstrated in Mircea Eliade's seminal work on the spread of Shamanism.

Yet the philosophical unity in the concept of Shiva is not breached or violated by these contrary and often contradictory visions. The dreaming god of the mountains continues to hold the entirety of the created and uncreated world in the inner vision of his third eye.

The Manifestations of Shiva

Shiva's manifestations are complex and contradictory, for he is the all-encompassing reality who resolves all polarities in his being. His auspicious and terrible aspects are all mirrors of the same primary self.

Shiva is the god who must not be named, for to name is to limit and curtail; yet his many names together constitute the sum of his unknowable mysteries. The many realities of the multifaceted Shiva are encompassed by the aspects described in his different manifestations. These constitute a poetic, mythic rendering of the world-reality, a sakshat or saguna naming of the unnameable, inscrutable mysteries of the nirguna or unqualified godhead.

Rudra: In the Vedas, Shiva appears as Rudra, the howler. He is the embodiment of the 'Great Fear', of the thunderbolt. Harbinger of both rain and prosperity, he is entirely fearful in his terrible beauty. Raudra or Rudra is he whose name is not uttered, the Wild God of the Rig Veda, the First One, the god who is invoked by what one commentator refers to as a 'lucid frenzy'. As Rudra came into being, he brought the mysteries of creation and the manifest with him. When he approached, he howled (arodit), and so came to be known as Rudra, the roarer. In his manifestation as the lord of the thunderbolts, he encompasses Agni, the element of fire. Like Agni, he both sustains and destroys life. In the primordial and timeless moment of creation, Agni brought forth the seed of heaven, through Prajapati, the first Father.

As Rudra, is associated then, as now, with Agni, so is he associated with Bhairava, the destructive aspect of Rudra. He is also the embodiment of the sun, the element of cosmic fire, and in this form his son is the planet Saturn, born of his wife Survarchala. As Rudra is among the solar divinities, he is invoked as Bhuteshvara, the lord of elements. Later the bhutas came to be perceived as ghosts and spirits, and consequently Bhuteshvara became the god of spirits and ghosts. In his aspect as Bhuteshvara, Rudra-Shiva frequents the cremation grounds, where, besmeared by the bhasma, a word connoting both destruction and ashes, he contemplates the continuity of death and life, of being and non-being. He wears a garland of skulls and, encircled by serpents, another potent symbol of cosmic continuity, holds ascendancy over the hierarchy of imps, goblins and demons that thrive in the dark aspect of consciousness.

The polarity of Rudra-Shiva, of the destructive and benevolent realities of the godhead, became embodied in the Ashtamurti, the eight aspects of Shiva. Of these eight names, Rudra, Sarva, Ugra or Ashani and Bhima refer to his destructive aspect, and Bhava, Pashupati, Mahadeva and Ishana to the benevolent aspect. None of these versions is complete in itself, for only when they conjoin do the magnificent forces of creation and destruction become manifest.

Sarva: After Rudra, the next aspect of Shiva is Sarva, the archer. Sarva represents the element earth, or Prithivi. As the son of Earth, Bhumi, he is called Bhauma, the earth god. His consort and feminine energy is Dharani, she who sustains. Their son is Mangala, the planet Mars. The word Sarva is derived from 'saru', meaning arrow. This arrow has three parts and is joined with Kalagni, the fire of destruction. The dispassionate mercilessness, the cruelty almost, of this manifestation of Shiva is difficult to understand for those brought up and trained in the simple polarities of good and evil. The arrow is a metaphor of Shiva's power, a parallel to the shaft of lightning which is the visible symbol of Rudra's wrath. These are the symbols natural within a hunter-gatherer and agricultural economy, but the metaphysical validity of their perception is an eternal and enduring one.

According to Hindu myth, at the inception of creation, Prajapati, the manifestation of Brahma the creator, violated his own daughter personified in the constellation Rohini (also identified with the constellation Aldebaran). This is understood philosophically as the violation of the ultimate and absolute reality, or the devolution of the unmanifest into the manifest. The great god Shiva, himself the ultimate and inviolable reality, through his manifestation as Sarva the Archer, aimed his divine arrow at Brahma-Prajapati, the father of the universe, and decapitated him, for the absolution of which he had to later suffer much penance.

The syllable Om is the bow, the Atman (self) is the arrow, Brahman (the ultimate reality) is the target. Carefully should it be pierced; thus one becomes united with it; with the arrow, with its target.

There is also a fascinating association of Sarva-Rudra-Shiva, of the Wild Archer, with Sirius, the Dog Star, the hound of heaven. When the sun of the vernal equinox arose in the constellation Rohini, he was the star Mrgavyadha, the archer who is the hunter of the antelope, the arrows his rays.

Whatever destroys any existing thing, moveable or stationary, at any time, is Sarva-Rudra. Sarva, as a name and form of Rudra, is invoked together with Yama, the god of death, and with Mrityu, death itself. And yet, in the spirit of contradiction and reconciliation that epitomizes Hindu metaphysics, he is also invoked in the form of

Bhava, existence. The divine archer holds the power of life and death, and these are not contrary but integrated aspects of his reality. He can avert or restrain his arrows, and through this grace he can liberate from death.

Ugra: The other malefic aspects of Rudra-Shiva include Ugra, the fearful, also called Ashani, the thunderbolt, the spark that conflagrates the fire of eternal destruction. His wife or consort-energy is Diksha, and their son is Santana or libation. In this aspect Ugra-Bhima-Ashani is the devourer of devotions, and the granter of all desires. Bhima represents the element of ether, and his consort Disha is the embodiment of the directions of space. Their son, Sarga, is representative of creation.

Pashupati: Shiva in his benign form appears as Pashupati, the herdsman, as well as Bhava, Mahadeva and Ishana. The Bhava aspect of Rudra-Shiva, the manifestation as existence, is associated with the element of water. Bhava is also recognized as Parjanya, the lord of rain. His consort is Uma and their son is the planet Shukra, or Venus.

As Pashupati, the deity is the embodiment of the fire element. In this aspect, he is the feeder of sacrifices, and his consort and feminine energy is Svaha, the goddess of invocation and propitiation during the fire ritual. Their son is Skanda, the god of war. Literally translated, Pashupati is the lord of the animals, a figure of protection in a pastoral economy. All beings in the manifest world, from the first being, the creator himself, to all others in the hierarchy of life, were his to be slain or protected. Shiva is the great liberator who unties the snares (pasha) of each pashu, of each individual life.

In the course of time he transmutes into Vastospati, the keeper of the Vaastu mysteries. Due to his association with the fire sacrifice, Rudra-Pashupati is called Vastvaya, a remainder of the sacrifice (vaastu) which remains even after the oblations have been made. This is not as arcane as it sounds, for it represents the material residue of the spiritual sacrifice.

Ishana: As Ishana, the deity is the embodiment of the element of air, and as such the nourisher of life. As Mahadeva, the great god, Shiva is represented as a priapic figure, the god with the lingam, the phallus, as his emblem. The lingam is the reproductive power that ensures the continuity of life. Shiva's semen is preserved in the chalice of the moon, and the life-force that sustains the cycle of creation is contained in him. In this aspect, his consort is Rohini, and their son the planet Mercury.

Shiva as Mahakala

Shiva as Mahakala is portrayed as Bhairava, the terrifying aspect of Rudra-Shiva. In mythology, Bhairava is so fierce that even Kala, who is the very representation of time and death, became fearful of him. So he became Kala-Bhairava, who is also Kala-Purusha, the controller of time, and Kala-Raja, its ruler, to whom time itself is subject.

Another important aspect of Shiva-Rudra is Mrityunjaya, who personifies the victory over untimely death. Pashupati, the lord of the animals, and Mrityunjaya, the liberator from death are benevolent aspects of Shiva in the Kala-Mahakala axis. Rudra was the bearer of the seed for Prajapati, the great father, and as the catalyst between the forces of the formless and the manifest, he is paradoxically both the ally and the opponent of time. Time is personified in Hindu religion and culture as Kala. According to legend, Rudra met Kala, the god of time, and in him recognized his own self, although time had only four faces and lacked the fifth face of Shiva, that which is beyond time, as personified in his transcendent aspect of Ishana.

Shiva is thus simultaneously both the personification of time as Kala, and beyond the limitations of time as Mahakala. As the Divine Archer, as Sarva, he represents linear time. The span of life (ayus) is the lived dimension of time, the duration of which the Divine Archer dictates.

Another name for the god of time, for Kala, is Antaka, the ender, who bends the span of given linear time to the unending cycle of life and death. Yet as Rudra he is the vital breath and energy, the prana that is the inspiration of life. The lived life is constituted of the rhythmic movement of prana, of the life breath, which is the manifest life-force. The mysteries of day and night, the cycle of the seasons, are all elaborations of this dance of time and life.

Spatial time was represented by Prajapati, and the myth of Prajapati and his celestial trials is worth recording and examining. Prajapati, the antelope, was pierced by Rudra's arrow. The wounded antelope fled to the sky and became Mrgasirsa, also identified as Orion. The metaphysical explanation is that Prajapati was pierced by Rudra's arrow and so abandoned his body, for 'the body is a mere dwelling place'. Prajapati's sacrifice led to his identification with the annual cycle, with the solar year. He was renewed each spring, at the vernal equinox, when Orion rose to herald the rising sun. Then, with the passage of time, the sun moved away and rose in another star, Aldebaran. This alteration in the sky-map, this celestial change of guard of the equinoxes, was translated in the mythic imagination into the image of Prajapati moving towards Rohini, as the father of the universe was driven by desire to violate his own daughter.

Astronomical time, the vegetative cycle, is all part of the temporal and transcendent cycle of life. Shiva is thus described as the maker of time, Kalakara, and 'he unto whom the beginning and end of the universe is gathered'. He is both of and beyond time, the point where the motionless time of eternity enters the arena of creation.

The distinction between Kala and Mahakala, between manifest and transcendent time, is a philosophical concept of great depth and magnitude. Time in creation is rhythmic, and this is why Shiva is understood as the cosmic dancer.

Another aspect of the Kala-Mahakala imagery is the concept of Sthanu, the great pillar, wherein, personified as Shiva the great yogi, time stands still, in deference to his meditations. The seeming paradox of alternating activity and withdrawal, of systole and diastole, of inward and outward breath, encompasses the dual nature of Kala and Mahakala. The mythopoeic mind uses allegory and symbol to describe conceptual and quantum reality. In the course of cosmic history, at the time of the churning of the oceans, the samudra manthan, Shiva swallowed the poison which had been thrown up by Vasuki, the king of the serpents of the nether world. The serpent is of course another analogue for both time and eternity, and Vasuki is another form of Ananta Nag, the cosmic serpent representative of eternal time, from whom the Kalakuta, the poison of tyrannical temporal time, rose forth.

All these images, of the great archer, the cosmic dancer, the eternal serpent, accord Shiva a place in the highest possible metaphysical levels. They represent the collective dreaming of an intelligent and evolved society that could instinctively grasp and understand great and eternally valid truths in a symbolic or poetic form.

VISHNU NARAYANA

The Supreme God of the Hindus is Brahman, the Absolute Universal Soul. The entire cosmos is a manifestation of him and it is from him that all forms of life evolved. He is formless, without qualities, neither male nor female, and infinite, without beginning or end. He is found within us and around us, and the goal of every Hindu is to shake off the karmic cycle of birth, death and rebirth and attain moksha (nirvana or liberation), which is unity with the Supreme Soul.

To make the formless or Nirguna Brahman comprehensible to the average person, he takes the form of the Saguna Brahman with form and attributes. This is the great god Ishwara, on whom we can fix our minds, pray and meditate. When Ishwara creates the universe, he is called Brahma; when he protects, he is called Vishnu; and when he destroys evil, he is called Shiva. The three together form the Trinity or Trimurti who control the universe and its functions. But whereas Brahma the Creator is less an object of popular worship and is, rather, associated with the development of philosophy, Shiva and Vishnu claim large cult followings and, along with Devi and a few other gods such as Ganesha and Kartikeya, are the popular deities of contemporary Hinduism.

In popular Hinduism, Vishnu is the Preserver, the protector of the good and the guardian of Dharma, the law of righteousness and the moral order. He is Narayana (the resting-place of souls), Parama Bhagavata (the Supreme Being) and Aja (the Unborn One). He is benevolent and reigns in Vaikuntha, the highest heaven and the goal of the pious. As protector, he is regarded as a bhoga murti, one who rewards his devotees. In an age of materialism, this increases his popularity several-fold.

Vishnu may be depicted as standing or seated, astride or beside his vehicle, Garuda, the eagle. He may also be depicted as Narayana, resting or seated on his couch Adi Shesha or Ananta, the many-hooded serpent, in the primeval waters. He is generally four-armed, holding the shankha (conch), chakra (discus), gada (club) and padma (lotus), although certain forms of Vishnu may have more, or less, arms and attributes. His consort is Lakshmi or Shridevi, the goddess of prosperity, who emerged from the primordial waters, seated on the lotus and holding a lotus. Sometimes Vishnu is depicted with a second consort, Bhudevi or the earth mother.

The most important aspect of Vishnu is his ability to incarnate himself on earth whenever Dharma is in danger, to save good from evil. The incarnation may be human, anthropomorphic or animal. In popular perception Vishnu has ten incarnations, of which the last is yet to be born. Of the incarnations, two—Rama and Krishna—are the subjects of India's two great epics, the Ramayana and the Mahabharata, and command their own devotees. Their popularity has contributed greatly to the growth of Vishnu and the Vaishnava sect.

Vishnu

Vishnu is an ancient god who first appears in the Rig Veda as an Aditya or solar deity, the son of Aditi, the mother of the gods. Early Vedic religion was intensely pantheistic in nature and all the devas or 'shining ones' (the word would come to mean gods much later) were aspects of natural forces over which the people had no control. Vedic gods were generally solar in nature, the sun being the source of all life on earth.

The Rig Vedic Vishnu is a manifestation of light, whose head was, by a trick of the gods, severed from his body and became the sun. He is the creator of the solar year: like a rounded wheel, he sets in motion his 'ninety racing steeds and the four', says the Veda. Here the steeds represent the days in each season and the 'four', the four seasons themselves.

Vishnu's unique quality in the Rig Veda is his ability to stride through the universe in three steps. Man knows the first two positions where he places his foot, for they are the positions of the rising and setting sun. But Vishnu alone knows the third place, the highest point in the firmament, and the position of the midday sun. This is the abode of the pious dead to which his devotees aspire, the goal of all spiritual attainment. The dust raised by his footsteps forms the rays of the sun that envelop the world. By striding thus, he holds up the sky and maintains the cosmic order.

In the Veda, Vishnu is a friend and associate of Indra, god of rain, thunder and storm. Together, Vishnu the sun and Indra the rain, take on the demon Vritra, the drought.

Indra and Vishnu are alternately described as Vritrahan or the killer of Vritra. The story of drought in India is as old as Indian civilization. Further, this was a period when the river Saraswati in western India was gradually drying up and the desert was advancing. In the circumstances, the sun was invoked to unleash the rain and provide devotees with a bountiful harvest.

Vishnu is also the protector of the sacrifice in the Rig Veda. He is the sacrifice, he obtains its fruits, and he averts the evil consequences of defects in the sacrifice. In the Brahmanic period, when sacrifices became paramount, this was an important quality that contributed to Vishnu's position as the Supreme God. A story in the Shatapatha Brahmana describes how Vishnu attained the position of the Supreme God. The devas held a sacrificial session. It was decided that the deity who, by virtue of his deeds, completed the sacrifice first should be deemed the highest of the gods. Vishnu attained the end first and was therefore given the supreme position.

The Rig Vedic Vishnu is associated with the mountains, as girikshit and girishtha. This connection is not very clear, as the popular perception of the god is either pastoral or aquatic.

While most of the prominent deities of early Vedic religion were relegated to minor roles as the religion developed, Vishnu grew in popularity and strength till he became one of the most powerful gods of Hinduism.

His rapid growth in stature was due to his benevolent nature, the seed of which is to be found in the Rig Veda itself. Vishnu means all-pervading: he is the all-pervading sun, whose rays envelope the earth, who protects the sacrifice and sends forth the rain and is the final abode of the pious dead. He is invoked to bestow wealth, welfare, possessions and protection. He takes his three strides to secure his people. Benevolence, goodwill and willingness to help his devotees whenever they call upon him are characteristics that made Vishnu popular in an increasingly material world and which brought him into the world in several incarnations. His name Vasu itself means wealth, and he is identified with gold, the colour of the sun. He is also the lord of cattle, a symbol of wealth.

Along with Brahma the Creator and Shiva the Destroyer, Vishnu the Preserver became one of the Trinity and, for ardent Vaishnavas, the Supreme God Himself.

Narayana

An important aspect of Vishnu is Narayana, the resting place of departed souls. This quality appears in the Rig Vedic description of the 'paramam padam', the third resting place of his foot, the highest point in the sky, the goal of pious souls. Narayana lies on the waters. Out of his navel grows a lotus, on which is seated the Creator Brahma. When evil is destroyed after each yuga and the earth is plunged into darkness and floods, Narayana creates a new world and gives people the opportunity to be good again. He may lie on the waters represented by the multi-hooded cobra or, in the form of a small child, float on a leaf on the water.

Narayana is more complex than Vishnu. The name Narayana itself first appears in the Shatapatha Brahmana, although not in connection with Vishnu. The Narayana form of the god was unknown to the early Vedas, while his character evolves much later, in the epic period. The Mahabharata tells us that he had given the waters the name *nara* and as they are his abode, he is called Narayana. But water in Sanskrit is aapa. Neera or neeru is the common word for water in all the Dravidian languages. Again, ayana is described as abode. But the Sanskrit word for abode is ayatana. In the Dravidian languages, the meaning of aya is 'to lie' or 'to lose consciousness as in sleep', while an is the male personal termination.

Thus Narayana appears to be a non-Vedic deity with Dravidian origins who was combined with the Vedic Vishnu.

The Atharva Veda speaks of a great yaksha in the midst of creation, lying upon the sea in penance, with the gods set therein like the branches of a tree. This yaksha who knows the reed of God is the mysterious Lord of Life. This is the earliest description of a figure resembling the Narayana of later literature and of the tree of creation. Yakshas were non-Vedic gods and spirits connected with nature worship. They lived in plants and water and were popular in Buddhism and Jainism. Although they disappeared from later religion, they live on in local sects and traditions.

At the time of the great flood, the mahapralaya, Rishi Markandeya was traversing the vast expanse of the waters which had destroyed everything on earth. He came across a small child resting on the branch of a tree. Amazed at the sight, the holy sage asked the child to identify himself. 'Long ago, I gave the waters the name Nara. Because they have always been my abode, I am called Narayana.' Narayana then took credit for the creation, preservation and destruction of the universe. The motif of a child floating on a leaf is still seen in popular art. Many ancient Tamil tribes and dynasties claimed origin from this form of Narayana. These stories, along with other evidence suggest that Narayana was a non-Vedic deity of the waters who was combined with the solar Vishnu of the Vedas to form a composite God, who was to become one of the most powerful deities of Hinduism. The combination of the two—Vishnu and Narayana—contributed to the popularity and growth of the deity.

Vaikuntha

This is Vishnu's heaven, the goal to which all mortals aspire. It is the ultimate paradise where everything is perfect. Sometimes it is identified with Mount Meru, the centre of the universe, sometimes it is called the Northern Ocean. It is also called Vaibhra. Vishnu is the Lord of Paradise, or Vaikunthanatha.

The eagle and the snake

The Adiparva of the Mahabharata has an elaborate story to explain the association of the eagle and the snake with Vishnu and their mutual enmity. Kadru and Vinata, two daughters of Prajapati, were married to Rishi Kashyapa.

Granted a boon by their husband, Kadru asked for a thousand powerful Nagas as her sons, while Vinata asked for two sons, equal in strength, energy, size and prowess to all the thousand sons of Kadru.

After a long time, Kadru gave birth to one thousand eggs and Vinata two. They were kept separately in warm vessels for five hundred years, when the sons of Kadru were born. But Vinata's eggs did not produce anything. Ashamed, Vinata broke open one egg and a half-formed embryo with its upper part developed came out and, for prematurely breaking the egg, cursed her with five thousand years of slavery to her sister Kadru. Then the child became Aruna (dawn), the charioteer of the Sun, and is seen early every morning, shielding the earth from the Sun's heat.

Meanwhile, when the ocean was churned for amrita, the nectar of immortality (see chapter on Kurma, the Tortoise), one of its many products was the beautiful and powerful horse Ucchaishravas. Kadru and Vinata had a wager about its colour. Vinata said it was white, Kadru said it had a black tail. The loser would become the slave of the winner. Kadru asked her Naga sons to cover the horse's tail, that it may appear black. When they refused, she cursed them to die in the snake sacrifice that Janamejaya of the Pandavas would perform. Worried, the Nagas decided to become black hairs on the horse's tail, and Vinata thus became Kadru's slave.

Five thousand years passed and Vinata's second egg burst open, revealing Garuda, a bird of great splendour and strength, who soared into the sky in search of his natural food, snakes. But he, along with his mother was forced to serve the Nagas. When he asked the Nagas for the price of their freedom, they demanded amrita, the nectar of immortality. Garuda fought the devas and took away the nectar, but did not drink it himself. Pleased with Garuda's self-denial, Vishnu granted him immortality, freedom from disease and a position on the flag-staff of his chariot, above the god.

Indra granted Garuda's desire that snakes should become his food, and Vishnu took away the nectar when Garuda placed it on the ground. Thus Garuda freed his mother from slavery, the snakes became his food and were denied immortality.

Of the Nagas, the eldest, Shesha or Ananta, hearing his mother's curse, went all over the country, practising austere penances and meditating. When approached by Brahma, he lamented that his brothers had wicked hearts and were envious of Vinata and her son Garuda, so he desired to cast off his body and live a virtuous life forever. Granting him his wish, Brahma also commanded him to hold the earth steady. For upholding the earth, Ananta became Dharma. Ananta was so powerful that he alone could uproot the Mandara mountain for the churning of the ocean.

Ananta means infinite and represents the endlessness of cosmic time, while his thousand hoods represent the innumerable divisions of time. The word shesha means remainder and represents that which is left over from the previous creation, which forms the seed for the next.

Garuda the eagle is the vahana or vehicle of Vishnu. In the Rig Veda, he is an associate of Indra and the sun. The visual image of a huge bird with widespread wings flying out of the sky would have contributed to this association. Many civilizations have used the symbol of the eagle to represent the majesty, power and remoteness of the sun.

The enmity between Garuda and the Nagas is the enmity between the forces of light and darkness. Garuda and Aruna represent the sun and light, the Nagas night and darkness. Although darkness tries to swallow the light, light is immortal, giving and protecting existence. It is the divine Vishnu, the sun himself.

The attributes

Vishnu is usually depicted with four arms, though sometimes he is shown with eight or even sixteen. In his hands he holds the shankha (conch), chakra (disc), gada (club), padma (lotus) and, occasionally, the khadga (sword) and sharanga (bow).

The many arms of Hindu deities are symbolic of the gods' manifold powers. Whereas a mere mortal has limited abilities, a god's power is unlimited, represented by the many arms that hold a variety of attributes and perform myriad activities, often simultaneously.

Vishnu's attributes are of an evolutionary order, from the club (gada), used in hand-to-hand warfare, to the chakra (boomerang), a weapon that is thrown and from the shankha (conch), a war trumpet, to the padma (lotus), a symbol of creation and purity.

Vishnu's attributes were actually weapons of Rama and Krishna. The weapons are important in that they represent the evolution of the deity along with the evolution of the people who worshipped him. In fact, they are studies in Indian anthropology, with each attribute narrating a stage in the evolutionary process of the god and, thereby, his people. The contemporary celebration of the Ganesha festival in Maharashtra provides an interesting illustration of this process. Today's Ganeshas carry guns, kalishnikovs and nuclear-headed missiles, or sit in front of a computer. Similarly, Vishnu was given the weapons and instruments popular with his worshippers.

Gada

Vishnu's mace is called the Kaumodaki. It sounded like thunder and was capable of killing the daityas and was given to him by Varuna, lord of the waters. The name Kaumodaki is derived from the water lily plant, the Kumuda.

Of all weapons known to man, the mace or club is the oldest. Initially made from a thick log of wood and later of stone, it was the popular weapon of the Neolithic period. There is no civilization where it was not known: mace heads appeared in India as early as 10,000 BC in Mohenjo-Daro. The association of the mace with Vishnu suggests that the god would have been worshipped by a Neolithic people in the course of his evolution.

In the philosophical development of Vaishnavism, the mace represents the intellect, the power of knowledge and the power of time. Just as time is unconquerable, the mace destroys those who oppose it.

There are several names for the mace in Sanskrit literature, but the importance of the mace can be gauged by the fact that an entire book of the Mahabharata—the Gadaparva—is named after this weapon. The Pandava prince Bhima and his Kaurava cousin Duryodhana were experts in mace combat, and Duryodhana, the king of Hastinapura, was killed by Bhima's mace. Krishna's brother Balarama is also an expert in wielding the mace, and it is the weapon of Rama's monkey allies, the Vanaras. Gods and demons alike use this mighty weapon of war.

Shankha

There are several versions of how Krishna obtained his conch Panchajanya. A story in the Mahabharata says that Krishna obtained the conch after killing the demon Panchajana who lived in the depths of Patala (modern Hyderabad, Sindh). The Vishnu Purana and Harivamsa have different versions. After completing their education with Guru Sandipani, Krishna and Balarama asked their teacher to name his fee. Sandipani asked for his son Punardatta, who had been kidnapped by Panchajana of the Punyajana or Pani tribe from Prabhasa (modern Prabhas, near Somnath in Gujarat). Panchajana used the conch as a war trumpet (another version says that Panchajana lived in a conch under the waters). He had sold Punardatta to the matriarchal Naga Queen of Vaivasvatapuri (city of light) near Patala. Krishna killed Panchajana and acquired his conch, hence its name Panchajanya, and returned Punardatta to his father Guru Sandipani. When Krishna was identified with Vishnu, the conch became an emblem of Vishnu.

The Panis or Punyajana were traders, described by the Rig Veda as demons, usurers and even Dasyus (enemies) of hostile speech. They have been identified with the ancient sea-faring Phoenicians. Panchajana's aides, Hukku and Hulla, are described as speaking a strange tongue and having been brought up in a 'lonely desert far across the sea'. The Pani or Punyajana tribe had captured Kushasthali (modern Dwarka). By killing Panchajana, their leader, Krishna regained Dwarka. The acquisition of the Panchajanya conch, symbol of Panchajana, is symbolic of Krishna's victory.

The conch or chank shell is the shell of the gastropod *Mollusc turbinella rapa* which is found in the sea off Gujarat and in the Gulf of Mannar. A well-developed industry manufacturing shell jewellery existed as early as 2500 BC, while the conch was an article of trade. Later Vedic literature refers to the blowing of the conch at ceremonies, a common function even today, while the Ramayana and Mahabharata describe its use to assemble warriors and to create the atmosphere for a war.

The conch itself is not sacred: it is the divinity of Vishnu that makes it sacred. The story of Krishna's acquisition of the symbol from Panchajanya suggests that it was an emblem—like a totem—of the demon. As Krishna defeats the demon, he acquires the demon's emblem, again a totemic association, for the victor acquires the totem of the defeated tribe or warrior. The likelihood of a totemic association is reinforced by the fact that the conch is the symbol of the Jaina Tirthankara Neminatha, son of Samudravijaya, king of Dwarka in Gujarat. Each Tirthankara is identified with a totem-like emblem, an animal, a plant or a natural object (like the conch). Also, the shankha's association with the waters reinforces its association with Narayana, who rests on the waters.

In later literature, the conch is symbolic of the elements, derived from the separation of ahankara (egoism), or the principle of consciousness, into a twofold division of sense and elements. The vibrations of the shankha represent the material creative force. Apart from the five elements (earth, air, water, fire and space), three more properties are derived from space (akasha): mind (mana), intellect (buddhi) and egoism (ahankara). In Vishnu's hand the shankha represents space, a manifestation of sound, the origin of the elements and the creative force. It is one of the nine treasures of Kubera, the god of wealth, and grants wishes and wealth. It is used in the sacred ritual bath of the deity and in the consecration of a new temple and is blown during important festivals.

Chakra

As the gods and the demons churned the ocean to gain the nectar of immortality, Vishnu thought of his fiery and destructive chakra, which came into his hands and destroyed demons by the thousands. The Mahabharata says that Shiva created the chakra after he killed a demon who lived in the waters. Blazing with fire and energy, only Shiva could look at it, hence its name Sudarshana ('wonderful vision'). While there is no further explanation for this story, many of the tribes and asuras who challenged Krishna's chakra

with their own chakras were Shaivites. This could be yet
another instance of the victor appropriating the weapon of
his defeated enemies. According to another story, Krishna
worshipped Agni the god of fire, in the Khandva forest.
Pleased, Agni gave him the fiery Sudarshana chakra to
decimate his enemies.

The chakra is first described as a 'sharp' weapon of war
in the Rig Veda. But it is not a common weapon. Like
the shankha, the chakra is popular only in the epic period.
It is used by Krishna, the devas and the asuras. Krishna
used the chakra to behead the planet Rahu and the prince
Shishupala, to defeat the demons Madhu and Kaitabha and
to destroy the armies of Rukmin and Jarasandha. The word
chakra means wheel, although Vishnu's chakra is generally
translated as discus.

The distinguishing feature of the chakra is its ability to
return to the hand of he who throws it. Time and again it
is hurled by Krishna, destroys the enemy, sometimes entire
armies and kingdoms, and returns to him. Although the
chakra has been described as the discus, the only weapon
known to have this quality is the boomerang.

The boomerang is a Neolithic weapon. While the
aboriginal tribes of Australia are its best-known users,
several ancient people between Eritrea, Sumeria and
Gujarat used a boomerang-like weapon. The Sumerians
used a circular boomerang, not unlike the Pallava
representations of Vishnu's chakra. The Indian tribes used
both circular and crescent-shaped boomerangs. In India,
the Kolis of Gujarat, the Maravars and Kallars of Tamil
Nadu and some other Adivasi tribes used similar weapons.

Later, the Vishnu Purana identifies the chakra with the mind 'whose thoughts, like the weapon, flew faster than the wind'. The Bhagavata Purana describes the chakra as possessing the qualities of prana (life principle), maya (illusion), kriya (activity), shakti (energy), bhava (emotion), unmera (ideals), udyama (exertion) and sankalpa (will). The chakra is invoked in Tantrik rites, and a chakra held in a person's hand is the symbol of a universal emperor or chakravartin.

Padma

When Narayana contemplated the creation of mankind, a lotus sprang out of his navel. Seated on it was the four-headed Creator, Brahma, illuminating all the directions with his brightness. Narayana was given the name Padmanabha or lotus-navel.

The lotus that lit up the sky with its effulgence was identified with the sun. As the first creation of the Supreme Being Narayana, the lotus became a symbol of creation and, thereby, fertility. As it arose from the ocean, it represented the waters, the source of all life and also Dharma, the cosmic law. By growing away from the dirt and impurity of the sea bed in which demons and serpents dwell, the lotus became a symbol of purity. So also the individual soul, though rooted in an imperfect world, searches for perfection.

The lotus in Vishnu's hand also represents Lakshmi, the goddess of prosperity who is seated on a lotus and also holds one in one or both hands. The lotus is the creative force, generating cosmic action. It is the feminine principle that activates the creative power of the Supreme Being, like the yin and the yang or Shiva and Shakti.

Khadga

Occasionally, Vishnu holds the sword or khadga. However, apart from an allusion to Rama's sword in the Ramayana, there is nothing to tell us how and why Vishnu obtained it. It also appears very rarely in iconography.

The sword first appears in the coins of the Greek kshatrapas (satraps) of north-west India. Alexander's Greek soldiers wielded the sword and it obviously entered the country with them. Its association with Vishnu begins as late as the Gupta period, suggesting that its success in the hands of the Greeks made it a weapon to be respected.

Sharanga

Just as Krishna's shankha and chakra are associated with Vishnu, Rama's bow and arrow are also associated with the deity. The sharanga (bow) is not an important or frequently seen weapon of Vishnu and seems to have become his possession when the cult of Rama was identified with him.

Iconography

While the earliest extant image of Vishnu is probably a four-armed figure holding the shankha, chakra and gada from Malhar in Madhya Pradesh, dating back to 200 BC, Vishnu images are prolific in the Kushana period (AD 200). Most icons are four-armed and hold the shankha, chakra, gada and padma. His consort Lakshmi, represented as Shridevi and Bhudevi—the sky and the earth respectively—stands on either side of the god. Sometimes Lakshmi is also represented as the shrivatsa, a symbol of Devi that Vishnu carries on his chest. While the early figures are crowned or wear a headdress, later images wear the tall kirita, a symbol of divinity.

Standing images of Vishnu may or may not have Garuda beside him, but Vishnu generally sits on the eagle, just as he reclines on the snake, a symbol of the waters.

Later Vishnu icons are of three types: standing or sthanaka murtis, seated or asana murtis and resting or shayana murtis. Each may be of any one of four types: yoga for meditation, bhoga for giving boons, vira for the warrior and abhicharika for Tantrik ritual. The attributes he holds and the gods, sages and attendants who surround him, define each type. Each type may be further divided into three categories: highest (uttama), intermediate (madhyama) and lowest (adhama) depending on whether they fulfil all, some or none of the requirements.

The iconography of Vishnu as we now know him first appears in the Kushana period. But it was the Gupta period that saw a profusion of Vishnu images. Special mention must be made of the temple at Deogarh in Madhya Pradesh. Here Vishnu can be seen as Nara-Narayana, a unique relief of the duo of Nara and Narayana communicating, one listening and the other advising; as Gajendra Rakshaka (protector), a majestic image of Vishnu swooping down, seated on a flying Garuda, to save his devotee Gajendra, the elephant, from the crocodile demon. He is seated on his vehicle, the magnificent flying Garuda, and reclines on Adi Shesha, his bed in the ocean, with personifications of his attributes—the ayudha purushas—on a panel beneath.

Incarnations

From time to time, evil overpowers good and the earth comes to be ruled by wicked kings and demons who deny the rule of Dharma, the cosmic law of righteousness. They suppress virtue and morality till life on earth becomes unbearable. Only the truly devout survive and they put their faith in their god. In response to their prayers, Vishnu incarnates himself again and again as an avatar, to put an end to adharma, or unrighteousness, and restore order on earth. It is believed that he has manifested himself nine times, with the tenth or final incarnation yet to come. Some texts enumerate more, with the Bhagavata Purana mentioning twenty-two incarnations, but ten is the most popular number.

The avatars are, in order:

- Matsya, the fish
- Kurma, the tortoise
- Varaha, the boar
- Narasimha, the man-lion
- Vamana, the dwarf
- Parashurama, Rama with the axe
- Rama, the perfect man

- Krishna, the philosopher king
- Buddha, the preacher of peace
- Kalki, the final destroyer.

Each incarnation is relevant to the place, people and period. Interestingly, there is an evolutionary order among them, starting with the aquatic fish, developing into the amphibious tortoise, the four-legged animal and finally the two-legged human being. Besides these avatars or incarnations, Vishnu also manifests himself in different forms in different places. Each temple of the god has a unique story or Sthala Purana.

The incarnations correspond with the yugas or ages of life on earth. Each age is preceded by a period of twilight or sandhya.

The first four incarnations occur in the age of Satya (truth) or Krita (purity) Yuga, a golden age.

The next age or Treta Yuga commenced with the Vamana or dwarf incarnation. Sacrifices were carried out, and people were truthful and good. But righteousness decreased and people performed rites and gave gifts in order to receive rewards, not out of duty.

Dharma decreased further in Dwapara Yuga, when Krishna was born. Some men studied four Vedas, others three, two, one or even none at all. Disease, desire and calamities struck the world. Some people offered sacrifices to overcome them while others practiced severe austerities.

The last age or Kali Yuga began during the Mahabharata war. Dharma practically ceases to exist. Calamities and disease, poverty and hunger, violence and fear stalk the earth. The tenth incarnation of Vishnu, Kalki, will destroy the human race.

There is a difference of opinion as to whether Buddha was an incarnation of Vishnu, particularly since he was highly inimical to Vedic tradition. The alternative then is Balarama, Rama of the plough and elder brother of Krishna, who is listed after Rama, thereby removing Buddha and making Krishna the ninth incarnation. The inclusion of the Buddha was obviously done to integrate a popular school of belief into Hinduism.

While all other incarnations are partial—involving only a specific ability of Vishnu required to respond to a specific need—Krishna alone is a full avatar, the incarnation of Vishnu in his entirety on earth.

The promise of reincarnation has made it possible for several local deities to be identified with Vishnu. His numerous manifestations are the answer to every believer's prayer, for he sees in his local deity a form of Vishnu. As Krishna promises in the Bhagavad Gita:

Yadaa yadaa hi dharmasya glaanirbhavati bhaarata;
Abhyutthaanam adharmasya tadaatmaanam
srujaamyaham.
Paritraanaaya saadhoonaam vinaashaaya cha
drushkrutaam;
Dharma sansthaapanaarthaaya sambhavaami yuge yuge.

Which means:

'Whenever righteousness declines and unrighteousness prevails, I manifest Myself; For the protection of the good, for the destruction of the wicked and for the establishment of righteousness, I am born in every age.' (Bhagavad Gita, IV. 8)

It is this promise that the devotee sees Vishnu redeeming when he takes on a new incarnation or manifestation. This also makes it possible for a multiplicity of local deities to be identified with Vishnu and, thereby, be absorbed into the Hindu pantheon.

Matsya, the Fish

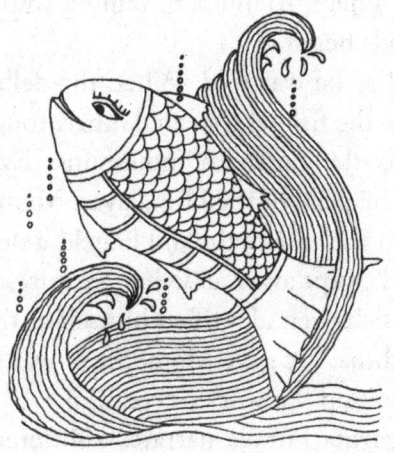

As the Matsya avatar, Vishnu saves Manu, the progenitor of mankind, the Sapta Rishis (seven sages) and their wives and one of every form of creation during the earth-destroying deluge. It is these survivors who later repopulate the world. Initially, in the Shatapatha Brahmana, the fish is identified with Brahma; later, it is regarded as an incarnation of Vishnu.

According to the Mahabharata, one day, when Manu was performing his religious rituals on the banks of the river Cherivi, a little fish came up to him and said that were Manu to take care of him, then he, Manu, would be saved from the deluge. He instructs Manu to keep him in a jar to protect him from other fish. Then, when he outgrows the jar he asks to be put in a tank. When he outgrows the tank, he wants to be taken to the river Ganga and, thereafter, to the ocean. There, Manu is to build a ship and board it when the floods begin.

Manu did as he was told. When the deluge began, he tied the ship to the fish who steered him through the violent storm towards the northern mountains. Eventually, the ship reached the peak of the Himalayas. Manu stepped out and descended the mountain and beheld a desolate world. The flood had swept away all living creatures: Manu alone was left. The fish then identified himself as the Lord of all creatures, Brahma. He gave Manu the power to create, and thus Manu took up the work of creation.

The Bhagavata Purana narrates a different tale. Long ago, when life first appeared on earth, a terrible demon called Hayagriva or Somaka terrorized the earth. He prevented the holy sages from performing their rituals and stole the Vedas, which he hid in the depths of the ocean. Brahma approached Vishnu for help and the latter immediately assumed the form of a fish and plunged into the ocean. He killed the demon and brought back the Vedas.

The Matsya Purana (named after this incarnation) contains yet another version of this story.

At the end of the kalpa (the duration of the world, or four thousand, three hundred and twenty million mortal years), while Brahma was resting, the demon Hayagriva stole the Vedas. When Vishnu discovered this, he took the form of a tiny fish. One day, when Satyavrata, the king of Dravida desha, was offering water in his cupped hands to the souls of his ancestors, he found this tiny fish in his hands. The little fish begged him to save it from the predators of the sea. Feeling great compassion, Satyavrata placed it in a pot. The next morning, he found that it had grown as large as the pot and thus, he ordered it to be placed in a well. The following morning it was as wide as the well, so the king transferred it into a tank. But still it grew, till it was as large as the tank. The king then told his men to take it to the sea. But even the sea was not large enough and the fish filled it from one shore to another.

Amazed, the king asked the fish to identify itself and explain why it was growing so large. The fish revealed himself as Vishnu and proclaimed that a great deluge—a mahapralaya—would flood the earth for a period of one hundred years. The king was instructed to keep one of each species of animal, all medicinal plants and seeds in a boat, with the Vedas above them. Thereafter, the fish told him to attach the boat to his fins with a rope made of a large snake. When the rains began, they came down so heavily that the entire world was submerged. The great flood continued ceaselessly for a hundred years. In all that time, Satyavrata and his boat were kept afloat by the great fish. Finally, when the waters receded, the creatures in the boat went back to creating new lives. And thus the world and creation began anew.

This story is very similar to the story of Noah in the Old Testament of the Bible, with the addition of the fish and the saving of the divine Vedas. The oldest recorded story of a great flood is to be found in Babylonian tablets. The story appears in the annals of every ancient civilization in Asia, Australasia, Europe and the Americas. It was obviously an actual event that has stayed in the memory of mankind.

At the end of the pralaya, Vishnu went back to his heaven Vaikuntha, without instructing people about the worship of the Matsya form or the construction of temples for it. Hence there are very few temples for this incarnation. The two best known are the Shankhodara temple at Bet Dwarka in Gujarat and the Vedanarayana temple at Nagalapuram in Andhra Pradesh. Matsya is generally represented as a four-armed figure with the upper torso of a man and the lower torso of a fish. Only occasionally is he represented as a full fish.

The fish incarnation also represents the earliest form of life, which began in water.

Kurma, the Tortoise

On the evolutionary scale, the next form of life would be amphibian, one that can survive on both land and water. This is represented by Kurma, the tortoise, the second incarnation of Vishnu.

The story of this manifestation of Vishnu appears in the Ramayana and several of the Puranas. Sage Durvasa met an apsara (celestial nymph) who gave him a garland that he, in turn, put over the head of Airavata, the elephant belonging to Indra, king of the devas. But the elephant threw it on the ground. Slighted, Durvasa cursed Indra that his kingdom and powers would be destroyed.

As their powers waned and they stood to lose their authority, the devas were afraid that the forces of evil, the asuras, would overpower them. So they rushed in panic to Brahma, the Creator, who advised them to seek out the Preserver, Vishnu. Vishnu instructed them to collect all the plants and herbs and cast them into the ocean of milk. Then, using Mount Mandara as a churning stick and the giant snake Vasuki as a rope, they must churn the ocean along with the asuras, with whom they should unite in peace. The churning would bring forth amrita, the nectar of immortality, that would restore their powers. The devas and the asuras did as they were told. But the mountain, being large and heavy, began to sink. So Vishnu incarnated himself as a gigantic tortoise, the colossus Kurma, and bore the great mountain on his back.

The churning of the ocean brought forth many wonderful things: Surabhi, the sacred cow; Varuni, goddess of wine; Parijata, the tree of paradise; the apsaras, celestial nymphs; Chandra, the cool-rayed moon; and visha, poison, claimed by the snake gods. Finally, seated on a lotus, came Lakshmi, the goddess of prosperity and the very epitome of beauty. With her came Dhanvantari, the physician of the gods, holding the immortal nectar, amrita, in a cup.

Both the devas and asuras were supposed to share the amrita. But, seeing the devas distracted by the appearance of Lakshmi, the asuras tried to steal the nectar.

Immediately, Vishnu took the form of a beautiful woman, Mohini, distracted the asuras, and took away the nectar of immortality, which he gave to the devas, thereby restoring their powers.

As in the case of Matsya, the tortoise first appears in the Shatapatha Brahmana as a form of Brahma, to create offspring.

Shrikurmam in Andhra Pradesh is the only extant Kurma kshetra, or temple of Kurma. Situated between the Vamsadhara and Langali rivers, it was originally a shrine for Shiva, and was later converted to a Vaishnava temple by the medieval preacher Ramanuja. Inside the sanctum, apart from the main image of Vishnu, the first icon to greet the visitor is a tortoise with an upraised tail, its back towards the worshipper. According to a local legend, a devout Bhil king regularly worshipped the image from behind the back wall of the shrine. Pleased at his piety, Kurma turned around and faced the king. It is likely that this story was created to explain why the tortoise faces west, because this is at variance with the scriptural requirement that the main deity should face east. It is also probably an instance of a non-Vedic local tortoise god of the Bhils being integrated into the Hindu pantheon by its identification with the story of Kurma.

The samudra manthan story is extremely popular in South-east Asia, where it is found in many temples in Indonesia and Cambodia. On the walls of Angkor Wat, Vishnu dances on the back of the tortoise, while the devas and asuras hold either end of Vasuki. But the most remarkable sculptures are to be seen in the ancient Cambodian city of Angkor Thom. The entrance to the city is made up of five gigantic gates, each representing Mount Meru. Each gate is mounted by four huge heads, each head facing a cardinal direction. Each deva and asura is a larger-than-life figure.

In Khmer iconography, the earth below symbolizes the tortoise, a partial incarnation of Vishnu, whose spouse is Mother Earth. The four heads which crown the peak of Meru represent the all-seeing Vishnu. He is depicted as multi-headed on the walls of the Bayon central temple of Angkor Thom, where the story is narrated in several sequences. Vishnu's ascent to the top of the churning rod is the representation of the supreme position of the midday sun, as it traverses the skies.

Kurma avatar is generally portrayed as a four-armed figure, with the upper torso of a man and the lower torso of a tortoise.

Varaha, the Boar

The boar represents the next step in evolution, a land animal and a mammal.

The Taittiriya Aranyaka and Shatapatha Brahmana tell us that the universe was formerly water, while the earth was the size of a hand span. Becoming a boar, Prajapati (Brahma) lifted it out of the water. The Brahmana gives the boar a name, Emusha. He was also the husband of the earth.

But the Ramayana and Vishnu Purana substitute Vishnu for Brahma when they describe the boar incarnation.

Kashyapa, a Vedic sage, married Aditi, Diti and the other daughters of Daksha, the Creative Power. Aditi gave birth to the celestial beings, the Adityas, while Diti gave birth to the demons, Daityas, including the terrible, Hiranyaksha and Hiranyakashipu. In a former birth the two were the doorkeepers of Vishnu's palace. But their arrogance had angered some sages who cursed them to be reborn as demons. They were incarnations of cruelty and caused great suffering to the people. Even the devas were harassed by them. Then, one day, the elder brother Hiranyaksha rolled Mother Earth up in a mat and threw her into the ocean. She let out a heart-rending cry that was heard as far as Vaikuntha. Immediately, Vishnu took the form of a gigantic boar and dove into the waters. There, he encountered Hiranyaksha and a terrible battle took place, in which the demon was killed. Vishnu then carried Mother Earth, cradled in his massive tusks, out of the depths. The devas and the sages sang in praise of the great boar. Varaha placed the earth on the ocean, where she floats like a ship and because of her massive expanse, does not sink beneath the waters.

The Puranas tell us that the boar was ten yojanas in breadth and a thousand in height. He was the colour of a dark cloud, his tusks were white, sharp and frightening. He was as large as a mountain, with huge shoulders and loins, and a roar that resounded like thunder. Fire flashed from his eyes, he was as radiant as the sun and strode like a lion. A veritable picture of majestic beauty!

The extrication of the earth from the waters also symbolizes the saving of the earth from the deluge of sin in which it was engulfed.

The boar incarnation appears in several inscriptions and sculptures of the Gupta period. The most impressive sculpture is found in the fifth century Gupta cave at Udayagiri in Madhya Pradesh. With a small Mother Earth seated on his massive tusks, the gigantic Varaha is indeed magnificent.

The town of Jhansi in Uttar Pradesh also has a famous Varaha temple, which is now in ruins.

But the most famous home of Varaha is the temple town of Tirumala, above Tirupati, also known as Varaha kshetra. At the end of Krita Yuga, Varaha was asked by his devotees to stay on earth and protect them. He agreed and sent for his divine garden Kridachala, which was brought from Vaikuntha by his mount Garuda and placed on the Venkata hills. And there he resides, with Vishnu's other manifestation, Venkateshwara. In fact, it is Varaha who receives the first puja and naivedya in Tirumala.

A little-known fact is that the period we live in at present is the shweta varaha kalpa (the age of the white boar). During the sankalpa, before performing a religious ceremony, the yajamana (performer of the ritual) recites the day, date, month and period, the last being shweta varaha kalpa. It is the same white boar that is believed to reside on the hill of Tirumala.

Another important Varaha temple is to be found at Shrimushnam near Chidambaram in Tamil Nadu, where Varaha is revered equally by Hindus and Muslims.

In the Tamil month of Masi (February-March), both communities take the bronze utsava murti in a grand procession to Killaiamballi village for a bath in the sea, as a re-enactment of Varaha's feat. The deity in this temple is credited with so many miracles that the name Varaha Saheb is common even among Muslims in this area.

While the fish and tortoise are represented with the animal forming the lower torso and the man the upper, it is the reverse in the case of Varaha. He is always a boar-headed man, with his four arms holding the attributes of Vishnu.

There is a myth that tells of Varaha and the Earth having a child, Naraka, out of wedlock, whose paternity is hidden from Vishnu by his mother. Naraka is an asura, the rich and powerful ruler of Patala or the netherworld, who is later killed by Vishnu. His paternity is revealed only at the time of his death. Naraka is the Hindu Lord of Hades, the result of being hidden away from the world above. In South Indian tradition, he was killed by Krishna on Deepavali, which is also called Naraka Chaturdashi and is the annual celebration of Vishnu's destruction of the forces of evil.

In Indian tradition, the boar is closely associated with water and believed to be able to predict the coming of the rains. Its ability to lift the earth with its tusks probably linked it with the tilling and ploughing of the soil, an agricultural activity. The story of Varaha is thus the story of the rescue of the earth from the all-consuming waters. Naraka, son of the boar and the earth, is identified with the Rig Vedic demon of drought, Vritra. As the boar ploughs and saves the earth, Vishnu conquers drought. It is a triumph of agriculture and man's ability to produce food. Deepavali comes during the monsoon season (November) in the south and is a celebration of rain conquering drought and saving the earth and the crops.

Narasimha, the Man-Lion

After Hiranyaksha was killed, his brother Hiranyakashipu swore to avenge his death. Although he was as evil as his brother, he underwent extreme austerities and received a powerful boon from Brahma. He would not die at the hands of either man or animal, not at night nor in the day, neither in the house nor outside, not on earth nor in the sky nor under water, with neither a weapon, nor fire, nor water. This unique boon made Hiranyakashipu savage and cruel. He denied the existence of the gods and took over the earth, the heavens and the nether world. He was inflated with pride and ruled the world with terror and fear.

Hiranyakashipu had a son, Prahlada, who was a devout worshipper of Vishnu. Whenever he was asked by his father to repeat what he had studied, Prahlada would sing the praises of Vishnu. This made Hiranyakashipu furious and he began to hate his son. He threatened to have him killed, but this did not deter Prahlada from his faith. Consumed by hatred, Hiranyakashipu ordered his demon hordes to attack Prahlada with their weapons, but the prince was not afraid of them.

Then Hiranyakashipu commanded the snakes to bite Prahlada to death. They bit till their fangs were broken and their jewelled crests burst, till there was fever in their hoods and fear in their heart. But young Prahlada remained unscathed. Hiranyakashipu then ordered elephants to throw down his son and trample him. But Prahlada continued to meditate on Vishnu and the elephants' tusks were blunted against his breast. A heap of wood was piled around the prince and lit, in order to burn him to death. But it felt cool and fragrant against Prahlada's skin. The prince was then administered poison. But this too proved futile. Hiranyakashipu hurled him, bound, into the depths of the ocean. But Prahlada thought of Vishnu and was saved each time.

Fed up, Hiranyakashipu asked him where he could see this Vishnu. To Prahlada's reply 'everywhere', the king kicked a pillar and asked him if the god lived in the pillar. Out sprang Narasimha from the pillar. He had a lion's head with a man's body—neither man nor animal. He fought the wicked demon and dragged him to the doorway—neither inside the house nor outside. It was sunset—neither night nor day. And then Narasimha, the man-lion incarnation of Vishnu, killed Hiranyakashipu by tearing his body with his claws—using neither sword nor fire nor water. Thus, Vishnu killed the evil demon without violating Brahma's boon.

It is said that so crazed was Narasimha at the sight of blood that the lion in him became uncontrollable and went on a terrorizing spree. The devas, even Brahma and Shiva, were unable to stop him. It was left to Vishnu's devotee Prahlada to finally calm the lion in the god and restore him to a state of tranquillity.

This is the first instance of an incarnation accompanied by an ardent devotee. The two are Narayana and Nara, one acting, the other worshipping.

The cult of Narasimha is extremely popular in Andhra Pradesh, Karnataka and northern Tamil Nadu where thousands of Narasimha temples, both big and small, are found. There are, in particular, thirty-two Narasimha temples in Andhra Pradesh that are important pilgrimage centres.

The most important is the temple of Roudra (angry) Narasimha at Ahobalam in Andhra Pradesh. This is believed to be the spot where Narasimha killed Hiranyakashipu. The pillar from which Narasimha emerged and the lake where he washed his blood-stained hands are situated here. So important is this shrine that the seat of the Vadagalai

(northern branch) sect of Vaishnavism is situated at
Ahobalam and the head of the sect is known as Alagiya
Singar (the beautiful lion).

The most famous temple of Narasimha is located
on the hill of Simhachalam, near the coastal city and
port of Vishakhapatnam in Andhra Pradesh. The deity
is known as Varahanarasimhamurti and is smeared with
sandalwood paste to cool his anger after the killing of the
demon. Simhachalam's importance grew from the fact that
Prahlada was believed to have lived and ruled here.

Other important Narasimha temples in Andhra
Pradesh include those at:

- Antarvedi where, it is believed, Hiranyakashipu's corpse
  fell when it was thrown into the air by Narasimha;
- Khaadri, where the terrifying aspect of Ugra (angry)
  Narasimha settled down;
- Anatavadi, believed to be a replica of a Narasimha
  temple constructed by the five Pandava brothers of the
  Mahabharata;
- Mangalagiri, believed to have been constructed by the
  eldest Pandava Yudhishthira;
- Penna Ahobalam, on the river Penna, where there is no
  icon, and only the footprints of Narasimha, measuring
  five feet by three, are visible for worship;
- Khamam, built by the Kakatiya rulers;
- Korukunda, built by the Chalukya kings;
- Singapatnam, where Narasimha is in the form of
  Shiva's Linga;

- Kondurg, where the image is in a cave in a hill, which has neither steps nor passage for ascent;
- Singarayakonda, the hill of 'King Lion' or Singaraya.

Namakkal in Tamil Nadu is home to a well-known Narasimha temple.

Holenarasipur, Saligrama, Konnakuntla and Karpara Kshetra are some of the important sites in Karnataka, although the most impressive is the massive Narasimha image at Hampi, the former capital of the Vijayanagara empire. Hewn out of a single boulder in AD 1528, during the reign of King Krishnadevaraya, the details of the figure and its ornamentation have been finished in intricate detail. On the base of the pedestal are carved the sun and the moon, testifying that the image will last forever. In spite of the broken parts, the twenty-two feet high colossus is an awe-inspiring and majestic figure.

Other important temples are those of Ugra Narasimha at Joshimath, Uttar Pradesh and Vidal Nrusingha Mandir at Nrusinghanath, Orissa, and the ones at Rather and Charthana in Maharashtra.

Narasimha is portrayed as a lion-headed man. Sometimes Lakshmi is seated on his knee, and this form is known as Lakshmi Narasimha.

The proliferation of the cult and the association of the story with several sites in Andhra Pradesh suggest that Narasimha was a popular local deity. Prahlada is believed to have been the ruler of Simhachalam and it is likely that the cult of his god Narasimha originated here.

Narasimha represents the beginning of the evolution of *Homo sapiens*, the transition from a four-legged species to man.

Vamana, the Dwarf

Vamana appears at the beginning of the evolution
of Vishnu; it was the twelfth [illegible] head [illegible] and [illegible]
[illegible].

Vamana, the Dwarf

Vishnu's incarnation Vamana resonates with the Rig Vedic
description of the solar deity who takes three strides across
the skies.

Bali, son of Virochana and grandson of Prahlada, and
therefore belonging to the Asura lineage, conquered Indra,
king of the gods, and assumed the kingship of the universe.
The gods were forced to leave Indra's heaven Amaravati.

To celebrate his victory, Bali conducted an elaborate sacrifice. Distraught, Indra and the other gods went to Vishnu for help. They asked him to take advantage of Bali's famed generosity and request the demon to restore the kingship of the worlds to Indra. For Bali was known to never refuse a supplicant.

Vishnu agreed to help the gods defeat Bali and regain the heavens. He then took birth as a dwarf, the son of sage Kashyapa and Aditi. He visited Bali's sacrifice in Indra's heaven. Bali was so impressed by the radiance of the young boy's face that he offered to give him whatever he wished—gold, houses, villages, food, drink, horses, elephants, cows and carriages. Vamana replied that a wise man should ask for no more than his needs, and all that he required was a small portion of ground, as covered by 'three paces measured step by step'. Bali's preceptor Shukracharya, the teacher of the demons, recognized Vishnu and advised Bali to refuse. But Bali insisted on fulfilling his promise, saying that he would rather lose his home than break his word.

So Vishnu took his three steps. With the first he covered the earth. With the second, the sky and the heavens. Then he reproached Bali for not providing him a place for the third step and condemned him to the nether world. Bali, who did not fear hell as much as he feared a bad name, offered his own head as a resting-place for the third step.

Vishnu placed his foot on Bali's head and started crushing him. But Prahlada appeared and pleaded with Vamana to spare his grandson, for he did not deserve the punishment. Vishnu relented and pressed down upon Bali till the latter went down to Patala, the nether world.

The germ of this story is to be found in the Shatapatha Brahmana. The asuras had won the earth and decided to divide it among themselves. The gods heard of this and wanted to regain the earth. They placed Vishnu at the head of the sacrifice and asked for a share of the earth. As Vishnu had taken the form of a dwarf (in this story), the asuras offered as much land as he could lie on. The gods accepted and thus acquired the whole earth.

In contemporary Kerala, the people believe that Bali was an ancient ruler of their land. After Bali had been defeated by Vishnu as Vamana, his subjects were miserable at his impending departure and begged him not to leave. Bali requested Vishnu for permission to visit his people once a year. Vishnu granted him his wish. Bali's yearly visit to his kingdom is celebrated in Kerala as the annual harvest festival of Onam, in the month of Chingom. It is likely that this story is an allegorical representation of the coming of the harvest and the offering of thanksgiving (bali) after a hot dry summer (the solar Vishnu).

Mavelikara in Kerala is the site of a famous temple of Vamana, locally known as Thrikkakarai. It is believed that Vishnu pressed King Bali into the earth here.

Vamana may be represented either as a dwarf or a giant with his foot on the head of a crouching Bali. A massive Trivikrama lifting one leg is sculpted in the early Chalukya cave temple of Badami in Karnataka.

A huge Vamana as the giant Trivikrama is the chief deity of the temple of Ulagalanda Perumal (Vishnu who measured the world) at Kanchipuram.

On the evolutionary scale, Vamana is an imperfect specimen, a dwarf. He thus represents the earliest *Homo sapiens*, who were quite small, as palaeontology has discovered.

Parashurama, Rama with the Axe

Vishnu incarnated himself as Parashurama to destroy the Kshatriyas, the warrior caste, who had become very arrogant and were constantly at war.

Parashurama, or Rama with the axe, was the fifth son of the sage Jamadagni and Renuka, and was also known as Rama Jamadagnya.

Renuka was a pious woman, known for her dutifulness and abilities as a good housewife. One day, as she went to bathe in the river, she saw Chitraratha, prince of Mrittikavati, sporting with his wife in the water. She felt envious of their fun and frolic and returned to her hermitage in a state of disquiet. Her perspicacious husband immediately sensed her mood and realized that she had lost her perfection and sanctity. Furious, he sent for his sons and demanded that they kill their mother. The first four refused, and were cursed by their father to become idiots.

Then Parashurama appeared. When confronted with his father's order, the dutiful son immediately picked up his axe and cut off Renuka's head. Pleased, Jamadagni offered Parashurama whatever he desired. The latter immediately asked that his mother be brought back to life with no memory of her death, her purification from all defilement and the restoration of his brothers to sanity. He also asked for invincibility in single combat and a long life for himself. Jamadagni acceded to all his wishes.

Now King Kaartavirya of the Haihaya tribe had been endowed with a thousand arms and a golden chariot that took him where he willed. But he was a wicked oppressor of the gods, sages and people. One day, he came to the hermitage of Jamadagni. In her husband's absence, Renuka received him with courtesy and respect. Instead of acknowledging her hospitality, the arrogant king took away the calf of her milch cow. When Parashurama returned home he saw the cow in great distress. On hearing the story, he challenged Kaartavirya to battle. He destroyed the thousand arms of the king and killed him.

To avenge their father's death, the sons of Kaartavirya visited the hermitage during Parashurama's absence and killed the aged and unresisting sage Jamadagni. When Parashurama returned and saw his father's murdered body, he was furious. He vowed to wipe out the race of Kshatriyas from the face of the earth. He pursued this mission with zeal stopping only when all Kshatriyas, including children, were destroyed.

While this story is common to the epics and the Puranas, the Ramayana continues the tale to tell us that Rama, prince of Ayodhya and the next incarnation of Vishnu, finally curbed Parashurama.

Rama was returning to his kingdom Ayodhya after breaking Shiva's mighty bow at the court of Janaka in Mithila, thereby acquiring the hand of Janaka's daughter Sita. Parashurama accosted him, since Rama was a Kshatriya prince and Parashurama had sworn to kill all Kshatriyas. Parashurama challenged Rama to bend the bow of Vishnu. Rama accepted the challenge and strung and bent the huge bow. Rama refused to kill Parashurama as he was a Brahmin, but destroyed all the wonderful abodes created by him. Parashurama was forced to go away and live out the rest of his days in the Himalayas.

It is commonly believed that this story is an interpolation in the Ramayana to acknowledge the divinity of Rama and his identification with Vishnu.

The worship of Parashurama is mentioned in a north Indian epigraph dated AD 200. The south-west coast of India—Goa, southern coastal Karnataka and Kerala—is known as Parashurama kshetra and is believed to have been retrieved from the sea by Parashurama. As he had killed numerous men, Parashurama had to undergo punishment and went on a pilgrimage doing useful things, one of which was the reclamation of the west coast. According to one story, it was a gift from Varuna, lord of the seas, after Parashurama shot an arrow into the water to drive back the sea. Another version says that he drove back the sea and cut fissures in the mountains (Western Ghats). He is said to have brought Brahmins from the north to this region, and the Namboodri Brahmins of Kerala claim to have come south with Parashurama. He is also credited with the construction of thousands of temples and the establishment of rituals based on the Sanskrit scriptures in this region.

The hermitage of Jamadagni, where Parashurama cut off his mother's head, is believed to have been situated in the village of Renuka near Nahan in Himachal Pradesh. The Parashurama temple is situated on the banks of the Parashuram Tal (lake). It is a popular site of pilgrimage and is locally known as Purani Deoti (ancient goddess).

Renuka Devi is also a popular village goddess of south India. She is represented by the headless figure of a woman with a pot in lieu of her head.

At Trichur in Kerala, the Vadakkunathan (northern lord) temple enshrines a small sacred dais called the Shri Moolasthanam, built in memory of Parashurama. It is said that before he disappeared, Parashurama gave his final instructions to the local Namboodri priests from this spot. He also promised to come back whenever they needed him and taught them some chants and rituals with which to call upon him. All was well for many years till a few young sceptics decided to test the efficacy of his instructions.

Parashurama appeared on the dais, furious. Cursing them, he disappeared, vowing never to return.

The Parashurama Devalaya at Nanjangud in Karnataka and the Parashurameshwar Mandir at Bhubaneshwar in Orissa are other important temples.

The Parashurama temple at Phede in Maharashtra has a very interesting story associated with it. A wealthy Muslim lady belonging to the Adil Shahi dynasty of Bijapur dispatched her ships filled with merchandise to Arabia. A terrible storm arose over the Arabian Sea. Fearful for the safety of her ships, she prayed to Lord Parashurama, for if he could subdue the seas and reclaim the land he could surely save her ships. Immediately, the storm subsided and the ships reached their destination safely. She built a temple in his honour in the village of Phede, which became a major pilgrimage centre for Hindus and Muslims.

Parashurama is generally described and portrayed as angry, hot-headed and uncontrollable. He is reminiscent of popular stories of the Stone Age man. Interestingly, even his battles were fought one-to-one, an axe in his hand.

Rama, the Perfect Man

The story of Rama, written by the sage Valmiki, is the basis
for the Ramayana, one of India's two great Sanskrit epics.
The persona of Rama is a role model for all Indians and the
story is popular in every nook and corner of the country. It
has been retold in every Indian language and has travelled
as far as East and South-east Asia.

Although the story of Rama has been narrated in every Indian and South-east Asian language, Valmiki's Ramayana is the oldest and the most authentic.

Rama was the prince of Ayodhya, born to destroy the wicked demons, particularly Ravana, who were terrorizing the earth and preventing the sages from completing their ritual sacrifices. To help him, the Earth incarnated herself as Sita, daughter of Janaka of Mithila, and the serpent Adi Shesha was born as Lakshmana, his brother and constant companion. The story is long but fairly straightforward.

Dasharatha was the king of Ayodhya in northern India. Childless, he performed the Ashvamedha or horse sacrifice. Pleased with his devotion, Agni, the God of Fire, appeared before the king and gave him a gruel that his three wives were to drink to beget children. In time, his first wife Kaushalya produced Rama, the eldest son, his second wife Kaikeyi produced Bharata and his third wife Sumitra produced twins, Lakshmana and Shatrughna. There was great rejoicing in the kingdom upon the birth of an heir. Rama's birth is still celebrated on the ninth day after the full moon in the month of Chaitra (March-April) every year as Ramanavami.

When Rama was sixteen, the sage Vishwamitra came to Dasharatha's court and asked for his sons' help in vanquishing two rakshasas or demons—Maricha and Suvahu—who were preventing the conduct of his sacrifices. Dasharatha reluctantly let his boys go. While they battled the demons, Vishwamitra taught them many spells and the use of arms. And when they finally killed the rakshasas, Vishwamitra took them to the court of King Janaka of

Mithila to bend the untamed bow of Shiva. On the way Rama released Ahalya, wife of the sage Gautama, from her curse. Long ago, Ahalya had had an adulterous relationship with Indra, who had come to her disguised as her husband. When the sage found out, he cursed her to spend aeons as a stone, till Rama appeared and liberated her.

Janaka had organized a competition for the hand of his beautiful daughter Sita, found as a baby in a furrow as Janaka ploughed the land. He declared that only he who could bend the mighty bow of Shiva would be worthy of his lovely daughter. None of the assembled kings were able to lift the bow, leave alone bend it. Rama tried and succeeded, winning the hand of the much sought-after princess. A message was dispatched to Dasharatha, who arrived with his queens. Apart from the marriage of Rama and Sita, Rama's three brothers were married to three other daughters of Janaka.

Upon their return to Ayodhya, Dasharatha desired to abdicate in favour of his eldest son, Rama. His second wife Kaikeyi, egged on by her maidservant Manthara, was very upset by her husband's decision. Manthara reminded her queen of a promise of two boons made by the king long ago, after she had nursed him back to health from a battle injury. Kaikeyi demanded that the boons be granted, and asked for the kingdom for her son Bharata, and Rama to be banished to the forest. The king begged, pleaded and demanded, but Kaikeyi stood firm. Finally Rama, when told of the promise, insisted it should be honoured. He left for the forest with his favourite brother Lakshmana and his wife Sita, both of whom insisted on accompanying him.

They reached the Dandaka forest and settled at Chitrakoot. Meanwhile, bereft of his eldest and favourite son, Dasharatha died of a broken heart, necessitating the return of Kaikeyi's son, Bharata, who had been away and was unaware of Rama's banishment. Bharata refused to ascend the throne and went in search of Rama, to bring him back. But the elder brother insisted on fulfilling his father's promise. Finally, Bharata took Rama's slippers to place upon the throne, agreeing to rule as regent till his brother's return after fourteen years. To expiate for his mother's sin, Bharata lived out the period as an ascetic outside the city.

Rama, Lakshmana and Sita had several adventures in the forest and killed many demons. The story of their travels is a geographical record of the Indian heartland. After ten years they reached the hermitage of Agastya on the banks of the river Godavari.

One day, Surpanakha, sister of Ravana, the demon king of Lanka (Sri Lanka), passed by and seeing the handsome Rama, fell madly in love with him. She asked him to marry her but he refused, pointing out that he already had a wife. Then she asked Lakshmana, but he too refused. Deciding that Sita was the obstacle to her marriage, she attacked Sita. Lakshmana jumped to Sita's rescue and cut off Surpanakha's nose and ears. Furious, she went to her brother Ravana and narrated the incident. Knowing her brother's weakness for beautiful women, she praised Sita's beauty till Ravana decided he had to have Sita. He told his minister Maricha to assume the form of a golden deer and distract Sita. Maricha tried to dissuade Ravana, but to no avail.

So Maricha went to the hermitage in the form of a spotted deer. Sita immediately desired the beautiful creature, and Rama went in chase, commanding Lakshmana to watch over Sita. But as the deer kept disappearing and reappearing, Rama realized it was a demon, and shot at it with his bow and arrow. As the demon-deer breathed his last he called out for Sita and Lakshmana.

Assuming that Rama was injured, Sita begged Lakshmana to go in search of his brother. Lakshmana drew a line in front of their hut and advised her not to step out of it while he went to seek Rama. The term 'Lakshmana rekha' (Lakshmana's line) has, in Indian culture, become a synonym for the boundaries of behaviour and decorum.

As soon as Lakshmana left, Ravana appeared in the form of a holy mendicant. He persuaded Sita to step beyond the line and give him food. As soon as she crossed the line, he forcibly dragged her into his magical chariot and flew off with her to Lanka. There he housed her in a grove of ashoka trees guarded by female demons and harassed her night and day to marry him. The virtuous Sita naturally refused.

Meanwhile, Rama and Lakshmana returned and discovered Sita's abduction. Crazed with grief, they went in search of her. They traced Ravana's journey by signs they found along the way. The first was the dying vulture Jatayu, who had fought Ravana while trying to save Sita. Then they came upon the Vanara (monkey) tribe whose exiled king Sugriva had saved Sita's jewels as she had thrown them down from the sky as signposts for Rama to find her. Rama killed Sugriva's brother Bali, thereby enabling Sugriva to regain his position and his wife Tara. While Rama was with the Vanaras, one of their tribesmen, Hanuman, became his ardent devotee. And it was he who flew to Sri Lanka to discover the whereabouts of Sita. The Vanaras then helped Rama build a bridge across the sea near Rameshwaram, in order to cross over to Lanka. A fierce battle ensued in which all the demons—including, finally, Ravana—were killed and Sita was rescued. Sita was then called upon to prove her chastity, which she did by entering the fire. Finally, the gods descended to vouch for her purity and Rama took her back.

The brothers and Sita returned to Ayodhya with their Vanara friends just in time to prevent Bharata from entering the fire, as the fourteen years of exile were over. Rama was crowned king and ruled justly and wisely for many years, ushering in a period of peace and prosperity. In popular tradition, his reign was the golden age of Indian history, or Rama Rajya.

A later interpolation in the Ramayana, the Uttara Khanda, has Rama banishing Sita from the palace because of the doubts of a washerman. She goes to the hermitage of the sage Valmiki where she gives birth to twin sons. She later sends the twins to their father's court to reclaim their heritage. Rama asks her to assert her innocence and return, but this is too much for Sita. She asks Mother Earth, who gave birth to her, to take her back. The earth opens up and swallows her. Rama then loses interest in life. Going to the banks of the river Ganga he leaves his body and ascends to his heavenly home. But there is no authentication for the Uttara Khanda, which was probably added much later when women were socially repressed.

Rama is, to Hindus, the embodiment of perfection. He is the perfect son and husband, the ideal ruler and, most important, the perfect man. Similarly, Sita is the perfect woman and wife, Hanuman the perfect devotee and Lakshmana and Bharata the perfect brothers. The Ramayana thus symbolizes the value systems of Hindu society.

Some scholars have seen, in the Rama-Ravana conflict, the clash between the Aryans and the non-Aryans. While many stories of the killing of rakshasas seem to confirm this theory, there is strong evidence to the contrary. Firstly, the Ramayana was written by Valmiki, a low-caste thief turned sage. It is highly unlikely that he was part of the ruling Aryan establishment. If Rama were decimating the tribals, Valmiki would not have made him the hero of his epic. Secondly, Ravana, king of the rakshasas, was a Brahmin, while Rama was a Kshatriya. So the Aryan-non Aryan confrontation is ruled out. Finally, Rama's allies, the Vanaras, were obviously a totemic non-Aryan tribe.

How true is the story of the Ramayana? With the limited archaeological evidence, it is not possible to answer the question. But the Ramayana is a book of geographical exactitude, with correct routes and accurate descriptions of local geological formations, whether it is the description of the bend in the river Narmada at Nasik or the height of the hill in Rameshwaram. It is highly unlikely that Valmiki the writer would have travelled the country to collect this information. Obviously, the knowledge was already available.

Also, Valmiki's Rama was human, not divine. The identification came later—Kalidasa's *Raghuvamsha* (AD 400) and a Vakataka inscription of the fifth century identify Rama with Vishnu.

Thus, it appears likely that a king called Rama did live around 1000 BC. The story is so geographically accurate, and so many places all over the country are associated with Rama, that it could not have been a creation of the imagination.

Rama travelled from Ayodhya in Uttar Pradesh to Rameshwaram in southern Tamil Nadu, so sacred places connected with him are found all over the country. The most important sites connected with Rama are situated in Uttar Pradesh, where he lived and reigned. Ayodhya, where he was born; Benares, where his devotee Tulasidas lived and composed the *Ramcharitmanas;* and Rishikesh, where a temple enshrines Rama's brother Bharata, are some of the major sites. Rama, Lakshmana and Sita lived for a while at the site of the Rama temple at Ramtek in Madhya Pradesh, while the Sitarama temple at Ahairi in West Bengal celebrates the release of Ahalya from her curse. Nasik on the river Narmada in Maharashtra, and Bhadrachalam and Parnashala on the river Godavari in Andhra Pradesh are other places that Rama visited. He met Sugriva and Hanuman near Hampi, the ancient capital of Vijayanagara in Karnataka. He received and crowned Vibhishana, Ravana's brother who changed sides, and worshipped the Shiva linga prior to the war in the pilgrimage town of Rameshwaram in Tamil Nadu. His footprints are enshrined here, on the Gandhamadana Parvata from where Hanuman started on his journey to Lanka.

These are just a few places connected with the story of Rama. There are many more, and an infinite number of temples—big and small—all over the country which celebrate this incarnation of Vishnu.

Rama is represented in many forms. He may be the ascetic with his bow and arrow, flanked by Lakshmana, Sita and Hanuman. This form is known as Kodanda Rama. Or he may be depicted seated on his throne, generally at his coronation, the beginning of Rama Rajya, a period of prosperity. This form is known as Pattabhi Rama (from pattabhishekha or coronation).

The Ramayana has been translated into every Indian language and the story of Rama is so embedded in the lives of the common people that his name is invoked at every instance, sung at prayer meetings and chanted during meditation. Even at the time of death, the body is taken to the crematorium and assigned to the flames to the accompaniment of Rama's name. For it is believed that when he left the earth, Rama took all the inhabitants of Ayodhya to Brahma's heaven, without them suffering death.

Krishna, the Philosopher King

If the Ramayana provides the goal of perfection, the Mahabharata, the other great epic, is the story of imperfect people and situations, and how Vishnu, as the incarnation Krishna, manages these contradictions. The story of Krishna has to be sifted out of the story of the enmity between two sets of brothers belonging to the Kuru family. But the Mahabharata is of enormous proportions. Several sub-plots and unconnected stories divert from the main epic. The story of each incarnation of Vishnu runs into several chapters. In fact, later texts such as the Vishnu Purana, Bhagavata Purana and the *Harivamsha* focus far more on Krishna, although the Mahabharata is the oldest and most authentic source. The Mahabharata vacillates between treating Krishna as a hero and as a god. In Puranic literature he is always a god.

If the story of Rama was long but straightforward, the story of Krishna is longer and meanders. The tale begins with Ugrasena, king of Mathura, who was childless. One day, when his beautiful wife was walking alone in a wood, a demon became so enamoured of her that he assumed the form of her husband. The result of their union was the demon Kamsa, an incarnation of the demon Kalanemi, son of Virochana and grandson of Hiranyakashipu (of the Narasimha avatar story). Kamsa had a wicked and cruel disposition. The earth groaned under the burden of his evil actions. He deposed his father and assumed the throne, proclaiming himself king and god.

Greatly worried by Kamsa's malevolent powers, the gods went to Brahma who directed them to Vishnu, who agreed to incarnate himself on earth as Krishna, son of Kamsa's sister Devaki, with his faithful companion Adi Shesha as his brother Balarama.

Now, Ugrasena's brother Devaka had a sweet-natured daughter Devaki, who was given in marriage to Vasudeva of the Yadava race. Vasudeva was also the brother of Kunti, mother of the Pandavas.

As the marriage party was leaving, with Kamsa himself driving his sister's chariot, a voice called out from the skies that the eighth child of Devaki would be his killer. Kamsa went to kill his sister, but Vasudeva offered to give him all their children if he spared her life. So Kamsa imprisoned Devaki and Vasudeva and had them guarded night and day. Six children were born to them, and all were slaughtered. The seventh child was the incarnation of Adi Shesha. He was transferred to the womb of Rohini, another wife of Vasudeva who lived in Gokul, and was born as Balarama. Kamsa was informed that Devaki had miscarried.

The birth of Krishna took place late at night on the eighth day of the second fortnight in the month of Shravan or Bhadrapada (July–August), celebrated annually as Krishna Janmashtami. The guards fell asleep and the gates opened. A voice commanded Vasudeva to take the child to the home of Nanda the cowherd and exchange the baby for the daughter just born to Yashoda, Nanda's wife. Vasudeva crossed the river Yamuna, exchanged the children and returned to the prison. The next morning Kamsa arrived and dashed the baby against a stone. But the child was Nidra (sleep) who rose into the sky and informed Kamsa that his destroyer was born and lived elsewhere. The enraged Kamsa went on a rampage, killing every new-born child in the region. Fearful for the safety of his child, Nanda took the baby away to Gokul where Krishna and Balarama grew up as brothers.

The story of Krishna's childhood is a combination of mythical exploits and childhood pranks and has created an entire literature and cult around Krishna. From babyhood to adulthood he is credited with the destruction of many demons sent by Kamsa to kill him, and with the release of heavenly beings cursed to live on earth: Putana the female demon was killed by baby Krishna, and the sons of Kubera the god of wealth were liberated by him from their curse. Other demons destroyed by him include the whirlwind demon Trinavartta, the crane demon Bakasura, the horse demon Hayas and the bull demon Arishta. All these adventures took place on the banks of the Yamuna. But the river itself was poisoned by the many-headed snake Kaliya. One day, when Krishna was playing with his friends, his ball fell into the river. Kaliya caught him in his coils, but Krishna expanded in size till Kaliya let go. Then Krishna danced on the snake, nearly killing him in the process, till the many wives of Kaliya begged for their husband's life. Krishna banished Kaliya to Ramanaka Dvipa (in the Bay of Bengal) and the waters of the Yamuna became fit for bathing and drinking.

Krishna also took on Indra himself. He advised the cowherds to worship the mountain Govardhana in Vrindavan, for the mountain was the source of their prosperity. An angry Indra attacked them with thunder and rain, but Krishna lifted the mountain itself to save his people. Indra conceded defeat and offered homage to Krishna. This story probably indicates the shifting of popular worship from Indra to Krishna.

There are also many stories of the pranks he played on his mother and the gopis, or cowherdesses, with whom he loved to dance. Much later, these tales formed the basis of a whole cult of Krishna and Radha, his favourite gopi. But this was a development of the medieval period. In early literature, he was married to Satyabhama, daughter

of Satyajit; later, after he moved to Dwarka he married
Rukmini, daughter of Bhishmaka, king of Vidarbha, as
well as other princesses.

Unsuccessful in his attempts to kill Krishna, Kamsa
invited the brothers to the annual athletic events at
Mathura. On their way, they were attacked by the horse
demon Kesin whom they destroyed. At the games, two
wrestlers, with orders to kill Krishna, descended on the
brothers, but were killed, while an elephant sent to trample
them to death was slain. Kamsa then ordered his soldiers to
attack and kill Krishna and Balarama, but Krishna attacked
and killed Kamsa himself. He installed Ugrasena on the
throne and took up residence in Mathura along with his
wife and Balarama.

Krishna was the protector of Mathura, but later moved
to Dwarka on the Gujarat coast. He defeated and killed
Jarasandha, Kamsa's father-in-law; Sunaman, Kamsa's
brother; Kalayavana, king of the Yavanas (Persians);
Naraka, king of Pragjyotisha (in Patala); Shishupala, the
reincarnation of Ravana and Hiranyakashipu, Pralambha,
Jambha, Pitha and Muru. He destroyed Saubha, the flying
city of the demons, and decimated several tribes such as the
Angas and Bangas. There is also a 'false' Vasudeva Krishna,
an identity assumed by one Paundraka, who was killed by
Krishna's discus.

The conch and the discus held by Vishnu are actually
obtained by Krishna. By killing the demon Panchajanya,
he obtained the conch, Panchajanya. By propitiating Agni,
the god of fire, in the Khandva forest, he procured the
chakra or discus.

Krishna's miracles are legion. When the Kauravas seek to disrobe and humiliate Draupadi in the court of Hastinapura, he makes her sari endless. He saves the Pandavas from the house of lac set on fire by the Kauravas. In the great Mahabharata war, Krishna gives the two sides a choice: one would have his army, the other would have him, but he would not fight. The Kauravas choose first and take the army. The Pandavas choose second and prefer to have Krishna, who assumes the role of Arjuna's charioteer, hence the name Parthasarathi (Partha was another name for Arjuna, sarathi means chariot driver). Needless to say, the Pandavas won, but not without a terrible war of death and destruction.

At the commencement of the war, when Arjuna declares his preference for renunciation over fighting his relatives and peers, Krishna reveals the Bhagavad Gita or divine song, whereby he extols duty without thought of reward as essential for the triumph of good over evil. The Bhagavad Gita contains the essentials of Upanishadic philosophy communicated in simple language and uncluttered explanations. As he delivers his discourse, Krishna reveals his Vishwaroopa or Universal Form, whereby all creation, the stars, planets, people, animals, plants and more are found to be within Vishnu himself. And Krishna reveals that he is not merely an incarnation, he is the Supreme Being himself.

Krishna's end is foretold, as was his birth. Some Yadava boys had, as a joke, dressed up Krishna's son Samba in women's clothes and asked the sages whether 'she' would give birth to a male or female child. The sages retorted that she would bring forth a club that would destroy the Yadava race. Accordingly, a club came out of Samba. King Ugrasena ordered that it should be crushed to a powder and thrown into the sea. But the powder fell on the shore and became rushes, while a small part of the club, which could not be broken, was thrown into the sea. This was swallowed by a fish, which was caught by a fisherman and the fragment was made into an arrowhead by a hunter named Jara.

When Krishna decided to leave the world, he thought he would save his Yadava tribesmen from the curse of total annihilation by sending them to Prabhasa. Unfortunately, they got drunk, quarrelled and killed each other with the rushes. Krishna and Balarama were unable to stop the massacre. Then a serpent crawled out of Balarama's mouth the serpent Adi Shesha, of whom he was an incarnation—and Balarama left the earth. Krishna was sitting alone in meditation when the hunter Jara mistook him for a deer and shot at him. When Jara discovered what he had done he was horrified, but was forgiven by Krishna, who granted him instant salvation. Then Krishna abandoned his mortal body and left the earth. Dwarka was the Yadava kingdom established by Krishna. After his death it was submerged by the ocean and the Yadavas perished with it (although later royal lines and communities claim to be Yadavas). Recent excavations in the sea off Bet Dwarka have revealed a fortified city conforming to the epic descriptions of Dwarka.

If Rama is an enigma, Krishna is even more so. The sudden transition from child to warrior to Supreme God has made him the most complex deity of the pantheon. This complexity has spawned a number of theories of the origin of the god, some fantastic, others very logical. There are certain irreconcilable problems in the character of Krishna:

- The child Krishna was brought up by the tribe of Abhiras (modern-day Ahirs) and is still considered to be their god.
- After Krishna leaves Vrindavan for Mathura, he never looks back. His parents are no longer described as Nanda and Yashoda. He is celebrated as the Vrishni or Yadava king of Dwarka, Vasudeva-Krishna, son of Vasudeva and Devaki. He is now a ruler and a consummate politician, and a friend of the Pandavas who he helps in the Mahabharata war.
- Krishna expounds his philosophy in the Bhagavad Gita. But there is an earlier Krishna Devakiputra (son of Devaki), disciple of the sage Ghora Angirasa and author of the Chandogya Upanishad. A line-by-line comparison of the two books reveals amazing similarities.

So, who was Krishna? Were there three figures—the child god of the Abhiras, the Yadava king and the philosopher—combined into one? Or were the king Vasudeva Krishna and the philosopher of the same name one, leaving the child god of the Abhiras as a second figure? Or were all three different aspects of the same deity, as the Puranas suggest? We will never know the truth.

In the conflict with Indra and Krishna's advice to the cowherds not to worship the Vedic deity, it appears that Krishna directly challenged the supremacy of the Vedic gods, his own cult becoming superior to theirs. Krishna was a heroic figure fighting evil men and demons. It is no wonder, then, that Megasthenes, the Greek ambassador at the court of Chandragupta Maurya, called him Herakles (Hercules).

Professor H.C. Raychaudhuri has established the dates of the Mahabharata and Krishna from the list of dynasties in the Mahabharata, which corresponds to the Greek versions and the Buddhist and Jaina traditions. According to him, Krishna lived around 900 BC. The archaeological findings at Kurukshetra also corroborate this date.

In the association of Arjuna and Krishna we see a reflection of the combination of Indra and Vishnu. One is the doer, the other the all-seeing Supreme, the duo of Nara and Narayana, as described in the Mahabharata. This combination is different from Rama and Lakshmana or Krishna and Balarama, where one is the god and the other is his companion Adi Shesha.

Temples to Krishna dot the whole country. But the most important are those associated with his story.

The most sacred shrine to Krishna is the Krishna Janmabhoomi temple at Mathura. It is a tiny cell beneath the ground surmounted by a huge temple complex. Near the temple is Rangabhoomi, where he is said to have killed Kamsa. A few kilometres from Mathura is Vrindavan, associated with Krishna's childhood.

The tales and traditions of Krishna form an important part of the local lore and culture of Gujarat, thanks to the saint-preacher Vallabhacharya who was an ardent devotee. The main temples here are on the island of Bet Dwarka and the main Dwarkadhish temple of Dwarka. Krishna left the earth at Veraval, having completed the task for which he was born. Although it is not connected with the story of Krishna, the temple of Shrinathji at Nathadwara is as famous as the sites of Krishna's story. The icon holds up an arm to greet his devotees. This image is believed to have been originally made at Vraja in the Himalayas.

Other important Krishna temples include Jagannatha of Puri, an obviously tribal figure, the temples of Vishnupur in West Bengal and the temple of Vitthala in Pandharpur in Maharashtra. Manipur, whose princess married Arjuna, has an important Krishna temple. Their importance lies in the fact that Krishna is believed to have appeared to devotees in these places.

Kerala's tradition of Krishna worship stems from the association of the Pandavas who are believed to have spent the last year of their exile incognito at Thiruvarrpu. Guruvayur, Mavelikara, Ambalapuzha and Kaladi (birthplace of Adi Shankara) have large Krishna temple complexes.

Udipi on the western coast of Karnataka is the home of the famous Udipi Shri Krishna temple consecrated by the thirteenth century philosopher Madhava. Before entering the temple, the devotee looks through the famous Kanakadasa kindi (window). Kanakadasa was a low caste devotee who was not permitted to see the image, although he spent many a night and day singing in praise of Krishna. Eventually, his devotion was rewarded, the wall cracked open, enabling Kanakadasa to peep in and look upon

Krishna. Saint Vadiraja later installed a window in his honour. Udipi is also the seat of the eight Pejawar maths, one of the largest religious schools dedicated to Krishna.

Krishna and Rukmini are enshrined as Panduranga Vitthala and Rukmani at Pandharpur in Maharashtra. An elderly couple—Jnanadev and Muktabai—had an only son called Pundarik who was selfish, led a dissolute life and was uncaring about his parents, who he sent out of his home. But his lifestyle made him both poor and diseased, so he became a wanderer till he met the sage Kukkut, who revealed that his strength and powers came from caring for his parents. Pundarik saw the light and rushed home to serve his parents without a thought for anything else. His piety brought Lord Krishna to him, disguised as a visitor, but as he was massaging his father's feet, he threw a brick outside and asked the visitor to wait on it. Later, he apologized when he found that it was Krishna, but the god pronounced his pitrubhakti (filial devotion) the highest form of devotion. The deity 'stands-on-a-brick' (Vitthala) waiting for his devotee Pundarik. The temple belongs to the Varakari Sampradaya school of philosophy whose greatest exponents were the saints Jnaneshwar, Tukaram and Namdev.

At Puri in Orissa, Krishna is represented as Jagannatha, accompanied by his brother Balabhadra and his sister Subhadra. The story goes that King Indradyumna commissioned the divine carpenter Vishwakarma to carve the images out of wooden logs. Vishwakarma agreed on condition of total isolation for a month. But the eager king could not wait and entered the workshop before the month was over. He found the unfinished images and had to consecrate them as they were.

But there is probably an earlier tribal association, for the images look very tribal. It is known for its annual chariot festival when the three gods are taken around Puri in enormous chariots (whence the word Juggernaut) with their aunt Gundicha, where the local people can worship them.

In the story of Krishna and the Mahabharata war we see the beginning of the internecine warfare that was to plague northern India for the next three thousand years.

Balarama

Some Vaishnavas believe that Balarama was the eighth incarnation and Krishna the ninth. This stems from their refusal to accept the Buddha as a manifestation of Vishnu.

But the Mahabharata and the Vishnu Purana say Balarama was an incarnation of Adi Shesha, son of Kashyapa and Kadru and the constant companion of Vishnu.

Balarama was born of an embryo transferred from Devaki to Rohini, another wife of Vasudeva. He was born in Gokul and was an inseparable companion of Krishna, as was his earlier incarnation Lakshmana of Rama. Balarama accompanied Krishna from Gokul to Mathura and took part in the wrestling competition, killing Kamsa's star wrestler while Krishna killed Kamsa himself. He too had miraculous powers and assisted Krishna in the destruction of the demons. He killed the ass-demon Dhenuka, the monkey-demons Dwivida and Pralamba. One day, his companions asked him to shake down fruits from trees belonging to Dhenuka, the ass-demon. Balarama obliged them, earning Dhenuka's wrath. The demon attacked him, but was easily killed by Balarama. On another occasion, the monkey-demon Dwivida annoyed Balarama who was talking to his mother, so Balarama killed him.

Balarama was well-known for his addiction to wine and his bad temper. Once, when he was intoxicated, he told the river Yamuna to come to him, so that he might bathe. The river refused. Furious, he threw his plough into the river and dragged her after him wherever he went until she begged for forgiveness. He also killed Krishna's brother-in-law Rukmin in a drunken brawl. Balarama had one wife Revati, who bore him two sons.

Balarama was an expert at wrestling and club combat. He taught Duryodhana, the Kaurava prince, and Bhima, the Pandava, to fight with the club. He did not take part in the Mahabharata war but on the day of the mace battle between Bhima and Duryodhana, he went to watch the encounter. Draupadi had sworn that Duryodhana would be killed by a blow to his thigh, so, as they fought, Krishna reminded Bhima of her vow. But blows below the waist were forbidden, so Balarama, disapproving of Bhima breaking Duryodhana's thigh, left the scene of the war.

Balarama is associated with the plough, which he often used as a mace in battle, hence his name, which means 'Rama with the plough'. He is also associated with the pestle and the club, a weapon which he was an expert at using.

Balarama's character comes out as straightforward, fun-loving and highly principled. Krishna's machinations are beyond his comprehension and approval.

He dies along with his brother and Krishnavatar comes to an end.

Balarama is enshrined in the Puri temple in Orissa, along with his brother Krishna and sister Subhadra. Separate shrines to him also exist at Gokul in Gujarat, Alwaye in Kerala and Imphal in Manipur.

Buddha, the Preacher of Peace

Considering the antagonism between Buddhism and Brahmanism, how, when and why the Buddha became an incarnation is a mystery. He is included in the Bhagavata Purana's list of manifestations, thereby authenticating his association. The inclusion was obviously an ingenious strategy to integrate a very popular religious cult into the mainstream Vedic tradition. While Buddhism, as a separate cult opposed to Hinduism, disappeared from the country, it is not certain whether Buddha's elevation to the position of avatar was responsible for this.

The Bhagavata Purana says that Buddha's birth was for the purpose of deluding and thus destroying the enemies of the gods. He assumed a mortal form in order to preach heretical doctrines in the cities founded by the demon Maya and in Kashi (Varanasi).

According to the Skanda Purana, the rains had failed for six successive years and famine stalked the land. Brahma approached Ripanjaya, king of Kashi, and asking him to change his name to Divodasa (meaning servant of the gods), told him that should he become king, the gods would shower the earth with rain. Divodasa agreed on condition that Brahma would assist him and all the other gods would leave the earth so that he could rule without any rivals. Brahma agreed and with difficulty persuaded Shiva to leave Kashi.

Divodasa ruled well, but the gods were angry at their exclusion. Shiva sent his messengers to Kashi, but they were so happy there that they did not return. Then Vishnu, accompanied by his spouse Lakshmi and his mount Garuda, went and settled in Dharmakshetra, near Kashi. There he took the form of Buddha while Lakshmi took the form of a female recluse and disciple. Garuda became Punyakirti, a disciple to whom the Buddha taught the various branches of natural and supernatural religion.

Vishnu, as Buddha, taught that the universe had no Creator and that there was no Universal Supreme Being. Brahma, Vishnu and Shiva were merely mortals like himself. Death should not be feared, as it was only a peaceful sleep. Pleasure was the only heaven and pain the only hell, and liberation from ignorance the only happiness. Sacrifices were acts of foolishness. Punyakirti spread these messages in the city, while Lakshmi taught the women that all happiness was to be found in the sensuous pleasures of the body, and that caste distinctions were a figment of the imagination. As Lakshmi was very influential, her teachings spread rapidly.

As a result of the Buddha's teachings, which corrupted the people and took them away from the performance of rituals, Divodasa became dispirited. Then Vishnu took the form of a Brahmin and visited him. Divodasa narrated the many instances by which good men had to suffer because of the power of the gods and asked the Brahmin how he could achieve final happiness. Vishnu told him that his insistence on Shiva leaving Kashi was the cause of all his troubles and advised the king to consecrate and worship an image of Shiva. Installing his son as king, Divodasa followed Vishnu's advice and worshipped the Shiva linga. Pleased, Shiva appeared and led him to his heaven Kailash.

After converting Divodasa, Vishnu, as Buddha, stopped his heretical teachings and disappeared into a deep well at Gaya.

But the Buddhist texts tell a different story and one that dates to an earlier period.

The Buddha was born (in 483 BC) as Prince Gautama, son of the king of Kapilavastu and his wife Mayadevi, and belonged to the Sakya clan. His mother died seven days after his birth and her sister, another wife of the king, brought him up. As a child, he preferred meditation to

play. So his father married him at an early age to his cousin
Yashodhara. Although they were happy, Gautama would
still meditate on the problems of life and death. The king
tried to divert his thoughts, but without success.

Three incidents took place when Gautama was twenty-
nine years old, which were to change his life forever. On one
occasion, he saw a decrepit old man, suffering and ignored
by his relatives. On another he saw a sick man, shivering
and covered with mud. On the third, he saw a dead body.
Gautama was shaken and felt that youth, health and
happiness were irrelevant if they were merely waiting for old
age, sickness and death. Then he saw a mendicant, one who
had renounced all desires and led a life of austerity. Deciding
that such a life was fulfilling and preferable, he slipped out of
the palace late one night and left to seek the truth.

Gautama's journey of discovery took him to Brahmins
and sages, through severe austerities and penance, none of
which gave him his answers. Finally, under a pipal tree,
he received enlightenment and came to be known as the
Buddha.

The Buddha then proceeded to Kashi where he started
preaching his philosophy. He travelled around the region of
Kusinagara, Kapilavastu, Rajagriha and Vaishali, exhorting
people to throw off the yoke of Brahmanic observances and
follow the path of right conduct. He converted his own
father, while his wife became his first female follower.
He lived till the ripe old age of seventy, when he attained
Nirvana in the city of Kusinagara.

Buddha's teachings were based on the Upanishadic
philosophy of the transmigration of souls or Nirvana.

Pleasure and pain depend on one's karma or actions. Existence is a misery, and death is not necessarily redemption. He taught four 'noble truths': pain exists; desire is the cause of pain; pain can be ended by Nirvana; removal of desire leads to Nirvana. He spoke out against caste distinctions and all those who followed his tenets became part of a great brotherhood. Rather than physical mortification or costly sacrifices, he taught that charity or love was the greatest virtue, leading to Nirvana. He did not speak of God or a 'Supreme Being'.

Later, Buddhist literature created an elaborate mythology around the Buddha. Buddha's victory over temptation was personified as the nullification of the attempts of the demon Mara (also described as the God of Evil or the Lord of the World of Passion) who tried constantly to tempt or kill him. Rama's battles with several demons including Ravana, Krishna's battles against an even greater number and Buddha's defeat of Mara were all part of a recurring theme: the triumph of good over evil.

Buddha's followers followed a practice of erecting stupas or tombs over the various parts of his body and later, those of his disciples and senior preachers known as Boddhisattvas. The stupas became the focus of popular worship and dot the eastern and western countryside. The main stupas are to be seen at Sarnath and Sanchi and the important temple is at Bodh Gaya. It is believed that the Buddha's tooth is preserved at Kandy in Sri Lanka.

As Buddha had warned his followers against worshipping his image, symbols of the Buddha, such as the pipal tree, his footsteps and the wheel of law were worshipped in the early period. Later, in the second century AD, the image of the Buddha himself was worshipped. In the absence of a god, Buddha filled the slot for his followers. To Buddhists, he was the sole god who came to earth to teach them the true path. To Hindus he became an incarnation of Vishnu, one of the many deities of the Hindu pantheon.

There is no doubt that Buddha contributed greatly to the Brahmanic religion he sought to cleanse. Sacrifices virtually disappeared from Brahmanism. Love and charity became ideals to be followed for a better future life for the soul, in preference to desire and sacrifice. Ahimsa or non-violence caught the imagination of the people, even to the later detriment of the country, making it susceptible to attack and conquest. His philosophy was the Upanishads put into action.

The Buddha's establishment of celibate orders of monks also had a profound influence. Adi Shankara, who probably lived in the seventh century AD, established similar orders in five different places. Although several religious orders came up all over India, the Shankaracharyas were to become the most powerful authorities of contemporary Hinduism.

Buddha's life and teachings dramatically changed the complexion of Hinduism. His invaluable contribution to this process undoubtedly earns him a place among the incarnations of Vishnu.

Kalki, the Final Destroyer

This is the tenth incarnation, which has yet to come. Kalki is expected to destroy evil and re-establish virtue, peace and prosperity. The age we live in—Kali Yuga—is named after him.

The Vishnu Purana gives a prophetic description of Kali Yuga.

In Magadha will come a ruler named Vishwasphatika, who will destroy the race of Kshatriyas and elevate fishermen, barbarians, Brahmins and other castes to power. Outcastes and barbarians will rule the Indus, Darvika, Chandrabhaga and Kashmir. The rulers will be wicked and violent. They will kill women and children and take away the property of the people. They will rise and fall rapidly, and will not be pious. While the devout are neglected, those who mingle with the usurpers will follow their example.

Prosperity and spirituality will decrease and the world will be depraved. Property alone shall confer status, wealth will be the only reason for loyalty. Passion will be the only bond between men and women, the latter being used for mere sensual gratification. Litigation will be successful by the use of falsehoods.

The earth will be venerated only for her mineral treasures, the sacred thread alone will distinguish a Brahmin (not his acts of piety). Dishonesty, weakness, subterfuge and threats will rule the day, gifts will be made on ordinary occasions, not on religious occasions. Marriage will be performed out of mutual consent (i.e. love) and a person's clothes will decide his status. Water from afar will be deemed holy (not, as it should be, all fresh water).

It further predicts that people, unable to bear this, will go back to living with nature and eating natural foods, exposing themselves to the sun, wind, rain and cold. Life expectancy will come down and decay will flourish till the human race is annihilated.

When Vedic practices and the rule of law cease to exist, and the end of Kali Yuga approaches, the child Kalki will be born in the family of Vishnuyashas, a Brahmin of Sambhal village. He will destroy the barbarians and thieves and re-establish the rule of Dharma or righteousness. But those who change their minds and behaviour will be given a fresh chance and become part of a new age of purity, Krita Yuga.

Sculptures and paintings of Kalki show him to be a man on a white horse, sword in hand. Worshipping Kalki is difficult, for he has yet to reveal his form.

Other Incarnations and Manifestations

Although Vishnu is popularly perceived to have ten incarnations the number of manifestations changes from Purana to Purana. A list of twenty-two names is to be found in the Bhagavata Purana:

- Purusha, the progenitor of all creation, the original eternal man, even the Supreme Being. It is also another name for Brahma.

- Varaha, the boar.
- Narada, the sage, who has a leading role in the stories of Krishna. Some Rig Vedic hymns are ascribed to him. He is described as a Prajapati and a son of Brahma. Narada invented the vina (lute) and was the chief of the gandharvas (heavenly musicians). He was regarded as a mischief-maker, carrying tales from one side to another. But he was also a great writer on law and the author of the Naradiya Dharma Shastra.
- Nara and Narayana, the duo of the human and the divine, the doer who draws sustenance from the Supreme.
- Kapila, another great sage who was the founder of the Sankhya School of Philosophy. When accused by the sixty thousand sons of Sagara (the ocean) of stealing their father's horse earmarked for sacrifice, he reduced them to ashes with a glance. But when Sagara's grandson Anshumat appealed to Kapila to raise them to heaven, he promised that Anshumat's grandson Bhagiratha would achieve this by bringing the river Ganga to the earth.
- Dattatreya, an incarnation of Brahma, Vishnu and Shiva, though primarily of Vishnu. He gave Kartavirya, a demon who worshipped him, a thousand arms. He had three sons, Soma, Datta and Durvasa, who also obtained some of the divinity of the Trinity. Dattatreya's three heads represent the Trinity, while he is accompanied by four dogs representing the four Vedas.
- Yajna, the sacrifice, who was personified as the deer-headed son of Ruchi and husband of Dakshina. He

was killed by Shiva's son Virabhadra at the sacrifice performed by Daksha, son of Brahma, and a Prajapati.

- Rishabha, a great king of yore, the father of Bharata and founder of Jainism. He was the son of Meru and Nabhi and the father of a hundred sons, including Bharata. Leaving his kingdom to his son, he led a life of severe austerities and penance, wandering through western India till his death. He was the first Jaina Tirthankara.

- Prithu, a king of the solar race, believed to be the first person to have been installed as king. He was the son of Venu, a wicked monarch, and was born out of the right arm of the corpse of Venu, who had been beaten to death for his wickedness. Prithu granted life to the earth, hence her name Prithivi. He granted her a calf and milked the earth for grains and vegetables, on which people subsist.

- Matsya, the fish.

- Kurma, the tortoise.

- Dhanvantari, the divine physician, who taught the science of healing, or Ayurveda. He was produced during the churning of the ocean. He is also listed among the 'nine gems', nine brilliant men of the court of King Vikramaditya who lived in 56 BC. (His name appears twice in the same list.)

- Narasimha, the man-lion.

- Vamana, the dwarf.

- Parashurama.

- Vyasa, the author of the Mahabharata.

- Rama.

- Balarama.
- Krishna.
- Buddha.
- Kalki.

Other Puranas include the following incarnations:

- Hamsa, the mythical swan. Who Hamsa was or what he did is not known.
- Mohini, a combination of Shiva and Vishnu, who charms the demons into forgetting the nectar of immortality during the churning of the ocean.
- Dharma, the learned and wise bull, who is also regarded as a Prajapati. He had numerous children who were personifications of morals, intelligence, virtues and religious rites.
- Sanata Kumara, the mind-born son of Brahma. He was a rishi and the author of a minor or Upa Purana, the Sanata Kumara Purana.
- Hayagriva, a form taken by Vishnu to recover the Vedas, which had been carried away by two demons.
- Mandhata, who established the duties of the various castes.

The Bhagavata Purana goes on to add that the incarnations 'are innumerable, like the rivulets flowing from an inexhaustible lake. Rishis, Manus, Gods, sons of Manus, Prajapatis are all portions of him'.

There are several manifestations of Vishnu unique to their regions. They contribute to the character and nature of the benevolent god who comes down to earth from time to time to help his devotees in distress.

- Vaikunthanatha is very popular in Kashmir, Himachal Pradesh and other parts of the Himalayan region. He has four heads: those of a man, a woman, Narasimha and Varaha. This form is worshipped in some temples such as the Hari Rai temple at Chamba in Himachal Pradesh.
- Ranganatha is the god of the island (aranga) of Srirangam, formed by the river Kaveri and its tributary, near Tiruchirapalli in Tamil Nadu. Here Narayana rests on the serpent couch with his consorts Shridevi and Bhudevi at his feet. The Srirangam temple is a principal centre of the South Indian school of Vaishnavism, and was an important centre of Ramanuja, the tenth century Vaishnava preacher.
- Varadaraja, the giver of boons, is very popular in the south and is the main deity of the temple of the same name at Kanchipuram in Tamil Nadu. While the deity's right hand blesses the devotee in the abhaya mudra, the left arm points down, palm facing outward, in a gesture signifying 'take'.
- Padmanabha is often seen on temple walls as Narayana, from whose navel issues a lotus with Brahma seated on it. The Padmanabha temple at Trivandrum in Kerala houses this deity, who is also the patron god of the former state of Travancore.
- Balaji or Venkateshwara, the deity of Tirumala-Tirupati. He is a benevolent god, believed to always help

his devotees when they appeal to him. Balaji is probably the most popular and definitely the richest deity in India today. The stories of his miracles are endless and draw multitudes of people. The crowds at Tirumala are proof of his popularity. Several new temples to Balaji have come up all over India. This is why he has often been described as the god of Kali Yuga.

There are millions of temples to Vishnu and his incarnations and manifestations all over India. Many are local forms of his incarnations, as described in earlier chapters. Only some of the best known have been described here.

Conclusion

Vishnu is as old as Indian culture. He is worshipped all over the country and has been a common ideal and force for regions as diverse as Rameshwaram and Vrindavan, Dwarka and Manipur.

The identification of Vishnu with the popular hero-gods Rama and Krishna has undoubtedly aided his growth and popularity. Rama and Krishna are the binding forces of Hindu culture, as they depict the social and moral values of Hindu society. The epics are known in every part of the country and form an integral part of the upbringing of every child. As manifestations of Vishnu, Rama and Krishna lead to the ultimate goal of reaching Vishnu's paramam padam or lotus feet.

The use of the arts—music, dance and drama—to spread the tales of Rama and Krishna has increased their popular value. People enjoy sitting through long nights of music and drama, puppetry and dance, all of which are utilized to spread popular Puranic stories.

Vishnu's ability to absorb local deities has also helped to enhance his acceptability. People and cults that would have otherwise stayed outside the pale of Hinduism were gradually assimilated into this popular religion.

Finally, the worship of Vishnu demands bhakti, prapatti and sharanagati—or, total devotion, surrender and no thought of any other god. These are the paths to moksha, that liberate the soul from the bonds of earthly life and desire. The jiva or the individual soul achieves this through service and faith, one in which there are no distinctions of caste or creed. In the rigid caste-dominated structure of Indian society, this is a defining moment, when the individual is set free to traverse a new path, a path that will ultimately lead to Vishnu.

DEVI

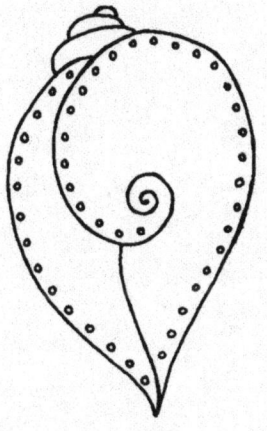

Hymn to Aparajita

'Salutation to the Devi, to the Mahadevi. Salutation always to her who is ever auspicious. Salutation to her who is the primordial cause and the sustaining power. With attention, we have made obeisance to her.

'Salutation to her who is terrible, to her who is eternal. Salutation to Gauri, the supporter (of the universe). Salutation always to her who is of the form of the moon and moonlight and happiness itself.

'We bow to her who is welfare; we make salutations to her who is prosperity and success. Salutation to the consort of Shiva who is herself the good fortune as well as misfortune of kings.

'Salutation always to Durga who takes one across in difficulties, who is essence, who is the author of everything; who is knowledge of discrimination; and who is blue-black as also smoke-like in complexion.

'We prostrate before her who is at once most gentle and most terrible; we salute her again and again. Salutation to her who is the support of the world. Salutation to the Devi who is of the form of volition.

'Salutations again and again to the Devi who in all beings is called Vishnumaya.

'Salutations again and again to the Devi who abides in all beings as consciousness;

'To the Devi who abides in all beings in the form of intelligence;

'To the Devi who abides in all beings in the form of sleep;

'To the Devi who abides in all beings in the form of hunger;

'To the Devi who abides in all beings in the form of reflection;

'To the Devi who abides in all beings in the form of power;

'To the Devi who abides in all beings in the form of thirst;

'To the Devi who abides in all beings in the form of forgiveness;

'To the Devi who abides in all beings in the form of genus;

'To the Devi who abides in all beings in the form of modesty;

'To the Devi who abides in all beings in the form of peace;

'To the Devi who abides in all beings in the form of faith;

'To the Devi who abides in all beings in the form of loveliness;

'To the Devi who abides in all beings in the form of fortune;

'To the Devi who abides in all beings in the form of activity;

'To the Devi who abides in all beings in the form of memory;

'To the Devi who abides in all beings in the form of compassion;

'To the Devi who abides in all beings in the form of contentment;

'To the Devi who abides in all beings in the form of mother;

'To the Devi who abides in all beings in the form of error; (Truth and error are both obverse and reverse forms of the Goddess.)

'To the all-pervading Devi who constantly presides over the senses of all beings and (governs) all the elements;

'Salutations again and again to her who, pervading this entire world, abides in the form of consciousness.

'Invoked of yore by the devas for the sake of their desired object, and adored by the lord of the devas every day, may she, the Isvari, the source of all good, accomplish for us all auspicious things and put an end to our calamities!

'And who is now again, reverenced by us, devas, tormented by arrogant asuras and who, called to mind by us obeisant with devotion, destroys this very moment all our calamities.'

(*Devimahatmyam*, 8–82, translated by Swami Jagadiswarananda)

Uma, Durga, Parvati, Lakshmi and Saraswati, are they one or are they different? When do they separate and when do they merge? Is Saraswati Vishnu's wife or Brahma's consort? When does Durga change into Kali?

If I had listened more carefully as a child to my grandmother's daily chanting, I would not be so confused about the goddess as she changes her forms, the colour of her skin, the expression of her eyes. I may have known from childhood the Devi's 1008 names. As I read the Devi Bhagavata Purana, made notes from the Devimahatmyam, searched for the real Radha and Sita in the epics, I came to understand better why Durga is also called Katyayani; how she turned into Kaushiki in just a fleeting moment; how she slayed the demon Mahishasura. Why was Shiva not invited to Daksha's great sacrifice? Why did Saraswati leave Vaikunth? These myths were retold over and over again as my grandmother chanted her prayers and sang to herself in that lonely hour of the morning. Her voice was jagged with age and sometimes she just hummed to herself, reciting the verses in her mind, or she would place her spectacles on the tip of her nose and read aloud from a heavy red cloth-bound book. I now know it was the Bhagavata Purana, a treasure trove of mythological stories.

The two great epics, the Ramayana and the Mahabharata and the Puranas are the source of most of the stories narrated

here, though I have included some popular folk myths too
which are not found in the Puranas. The main Puranas
like the Devi Bhagavata Purana sing the praises of the
particular god but they also contain stories associated with
other gods and goddesses. Many of the legends, like Sati's
sacrifice, are repeated in many of the Puranas but each one
has a different ending to it. The lead role is always played
by the god in whose praise the Purana has been compiled,
while the other gods and goddesses are given minor parts
to play. The Devi Bhagavata Purana deals mostly with
Durga's powerful image but we meet many other goddesses
in the legends.

Who would not be fascinated by the wonderful imagery
related to these goddesses? Fiery-eyed Durga astride a
golden lion; Saraswati resplendent in white along with her
swan; a glowing Lakshmi seated on a lotus in bloom; and
Kali with her frightening garland of skulls. The legends
that surround them are told over and over again and soon
these beautiful lotus-eyed goddesses are not just religious
icons but part of one's family. They laugh and cry, quarrel
with each other over petty things, they have fragile natures
despite their powerful forms. They are often jealous, angry,
greedy and plot deviously against their enemies but still
they need to be loved by their devotees. Then they appear,
splendid, glorious and benevolent, to dazzle us with their
all-pervading light.

Durga

Durga, the great goddess with a thousand names and innumerable forms, appears as Shiva's consort in many legends, intensifying his attributes. But she is also, unlike most other goddesses of Hindu mythology, worshipped as an embodiment of female energy. She is the formidable Devi and Mahadevi and has many other powerful independent female forms. In a hymn recited by Arjuna in the Mahabharata, her many names are mentioned,

'. . . Reverence be to thee, Siddha-Senani, the noble, the dweller of Mandara, Kumari, Kali, Kapali, Kapila, Krishnapingala. Reverence to thee, Bhadrakali; reverence to thee, Maha Kali, Chandi, Chanda, Tarini, Varavarini. O fortunate Kalyayani, O Karali, O Vijaya, O Jaya, younger sister of the chief of cowherds [Krishna], delighting always in Mahisha's blood! O Uma, Sakambhari, thou art white one, thou black one! O destroyer of Kaitabha! O sciences, thou art the science of Brahma, the great sleep of embodied beings. O mother of Skanda [Kartika], divine Durga, dweller in wilderness! Thou, great goddess, art praised with a pure heart. By thy favour let me ever be victorious in battle.'

There are several accounts of Durga's origin in the various Puranas. In the Vishnu Purana she arises from Vishnu as his magical force. He calls upon her to help delude a demon king who is threatening to kill the baby Krishna. She takes Krishna's place in Devaki's womb, saving him and allowing herself to be killed by the demon. Krishna, an incarnation of Vishnu, promises her that in doing so she would become 'assimilated to him in glory; she would obtain an eternal place in the sky; be installed by Indra amongst the gods; obtain a perpetual abode on the Vindhya mountains, where meditating upon him (Vishnu) she would kill two demons, Sumbha and Nisumbha, and would be worshipped with animal sacrifices'.

Durga is still represented, as she was centuries ago, as a golden-faced woman of great beauty with ten arms. In her right hand she holds a spear with which she is piercing the demon Mahisha. In her other hands she holds an array of formidable weapons. A lion, her mount, leans against her, its golden mane a contrast to her blood-red sari.

Idols of Durga in Bengal, where she is the reigning deity, depict the goddess with her four children: Lakshmi, Saraswati, Kartika and Ganesha. A small image of Shiva, her consort, is painted above her head. Durga Puja, an important festival of Bengal and other parts of northern India, is celebrated for nine days in autumn. The central image of Durga slaying the demon Mahisha is installed on the first day and verses from the Devimahatmyam are recited during these nine days. Buffalo and goat sacrifices were once a part of the celebration though now a pumpkin is cut as a ceremonial offering. Devotees sing, dance and feast, watched by the benevolent goddess and her family. Popular legends believe she is on a brief visit from her abode in the Himalayas where she lives with Shiva. On the last day of the Durga Puja, the idol is immersed in the nearest river with a great fanfare of music and dancing to bid the goddess farewell till she returns again the next autumn.

Though Durga Puja is celebrated in autumn, in some parts of rural Bengal she is also worshipped during spring. The reason for this is found in a legend from the Kalika Purana and Devi Bhagavata Purana, though Valmiki's Ramayana does not mention it.

Ravana, the king of Lanka, was a great devotee of Durga and worshipped her according to strict rituals every spring. Rama was advised by Narada to invoke the goddess since only she could help him win this battle. Time and again the mighty goddess has come to help the righteous.

All the gods in heaven pray to her when they want to defeat their foes. You too shall win this battle and regain Sita, who this evil Ravana has abducted, if you gain the favour of the goddess by worshipping her according to the method that is proper,' said Narada to Rama. The prince of Ayodhya then performed the puja in autumn since he could not wait for spring. The goddess transferred her favour from Ravana to Rama, helping him win the battle.

While instructing Rama on how the goddess should be worshipped, Narada tells him that the goddess was worshipped by the gods Indra, Shiva and Vishnu when they needed her help to defeat their enemies.

In later centuries too Durga was associated with military success and came to be worshipped by kings before a battle. Shivaji, the great Maratha ruler, is said to have received his sword from Bhavani herself. The founder ruler of Mewar, Bappa, according to a folk legend, received his sword from the goddess. After he had spent many days without food and water, wandering in the forest, the goddess Durga suddenly appeared before him on her golden lion and gave him a lance, a bow, a quiver full of arrows, a shield and a sword—a sword made in heaven by Vishwakarma himself.

The Markandeya Purana lists Durga's 1008 names. Many of these names are derived from the form she assumes to battle with various demons to save the gods. According to the Skanda Purana the Devi was named Durga because she slew a demon named Durga.

The Devimahatmyam, or the Greatness of Devi, forms a part of the Markandeya Purana. A poem of 700 verses, it is one of the main sources for the mythology of the

Mahadevi. This sacred textbook for worshippers of Devi in her forms as Durga, Parvati, Uma and Kali is recited in her temples and is known as the Chandipath. The following prayer is invoked during ceremonies devoted to the Devi:

'I resort to Mahalakshmi, the destroyer of Mahishasura, who is seated on the lotus, is of the complexion of coral and who holds in her (eighteen) hands rosary, axe, mace, arrow, thunderbolt, lotus, bow, pitcher, rod, shakti, sword, shield, conch, bell, wine-cup, trident, noose, and the discus Sudarshana.'

In this legend from the Devimahatmyam, the goddess, created by the light of three gods—Brahma, Vishnu and Shiva, assumes her most powerful form to slay the buffalo-demon Mahishasura and is thus called, thereafter, Mahishasuramardini.

A war between the asuras and the devas had been on for a hundred years and finally the king of asuras, Mahishasura, defeated Indra and became the lord of heaven. Victorious and full of pride, the king of asuras now assumed the powers of all the devas. He was not only Indra, but Surya, Agni, Chandra, Yama and Varuna. The vanquished devas wandered for a while like helpless mortals and then weary and tired they finally reached Vaikunth to take shelter with Lord Vishnu. 'See our plight, O lord. The mighty Indra is without his heaven, Surya has no light, Agni has turned as cold as water and Vayu too is still. Look how faded Chandra has become and Yama and Varuna stand before you as helpless as mortal men. Help us, O lord. Destroy this evil Mahishasura who has reduced us to this.'

When Vishnu saw his devas reduced to this sorry state and heard their voices full of sorrow, he was filled with anger. His face trembled and a fierce light shot from his eyes, straight as a lance. Shiva too appeared, enraged, with a great light, and then Brahma came and joined them, his face on fire with intense anger. From the bodies of all the other devas arrows of powerful light and energy shot forth. This combined concentration of light rose like a blazing mountain, its flames lighting up all the three worlds with a unique golden light. And then as the circle of devas watched, the light slowly gathered itself into a lustrous female form.

By that which was Shiva's light her face came into being, by Yama's her hair, by Vishnu's her arms, and by Chandra's her breasts. By Indra's her waist, by Varuna's her thighs, and by earth's light her hips. By Brahma's light her feet came into being, by Surya's her toes, by Agni's her three eyes were formed and the light of Vayu became her ears. The lights of all other devas too surged forward and they were filled with joy as they beheld the auspicious and beautiful Devi who had been thus formed.

Then Shiva reached for his trident and from it he formed a new trident which he gave to the Devi. Vishnu gave her a discus made from his own discus and Varuna gave her a conch. Agni gave the newly formed goddess a spear, and Indra, the lord of devas, brought out a thunderbolt from his own thunderbolt and presented it to her. Yama gave her a staff from his own staff of death, and Varuna, the lord of waters, gave her a noose. Brahma, the lord of beings, gave her a string of beads and a water-pot, and Surya bestowed his own golden rays on her skin so that the goddess shimmered in her own light. Jewels for her crest, necklaces, earrings, anklets and bracelets were given to her by the devas. Vishwakarma gave her a shining axe and the ocean brought for her garlands of everlasting lotuses. The mountain Himavat gave the Devi a mighty lion to ride on. Glittering with jewels from the milk-ocean, armed with an array of celestial weapons, shining with a divine light, the Devi gave a roar of laughter. As she laughed, stepping out from within the circle of devas, her mighty voice filled the entire sky. She laughed again and again making all the three worlds tremble. The mountains rocked and the seas churned with her terrible laughter. 'Victory to you!' cried all the devas in joy and the sages bowed their heads as she walked.

Mahishasura heard the Devi's footsteps which made the earth quake and looked up to see who was making all this commotion. 'I am the lord of this universe now. The sky, the earth and the oceans lie crushed beneath my feet. Who dares to make this terrible noise in my presence?' he said angrily and rushed towards the roar that was filling the sky and the seas. Then he saw her. The Devi stood pervading the three worlds with her lustre. The earth lay curved and bent under her footstep, her glittering diadem scraped the sky.

Then began a battle between the Devi and Mahishasura. The sky blazed as weapons were hurled by the mighty army of asuras. Hundreds of thousands of elephant soldiers, millions of foot soldiers, cavalry and ten million charioteers fought in this great battle. One by one, great asuras surrounded by scores of elephants, chariots and horses were sent by Mahishasura to battle with the Devi. They rushed at her with iron maces, javelins and spears. With clubs, swords and axes they tried to kill her. The Devi sat regal and still on her lion, bathed in her circle of unique light. The weapons the asuras hurled at her could not touch her, and she rode her lion through the battlefield, cutting them effortlessly. The lion's mane shook with rage as they stalked the army of asuras like a fire raging through a forest. While she fought, the goddess played on a battle drum and blew her conch to announce the victory which would soon be hers. Every time she heaved a sigh during the battle it would turn into a battalion of thousand men. The Devi killed hundreds of asuras with her trident, club, showers of spears, swords and stunned thousands of asuras by the noise of her bell and conch. Her swift arrows flew across the battlefield, piercing the asuras till they began to look like porcupines. Some had their heads cut off by her lightning sword while the others were torn into pieces by her axe. The battlefield was soon turned into a mountain of dead asuras, elephants, horses and chariots that had been felled by her. A river of blood flooded the earth as the Devi destroyed the vast army in no time. The generals of the army of asuras, astounded at how their mighty army was being routed, came forward to battle with the Devi, but they too were killed by her.

Then as his army and his generals were being destroyed, Mahishasura raged with terrible anger and assumed his buffalo form. He stormed into the battlefield killing everyone in his way with a blow of his muzzle. His hooves stamped the Devi's army to death and those who managed to escape were pierced by his mighty horns. Very soon Mahishasura had laid low the Devi's army and charged towards her lion. Pounding the earth with his hooves, Mahishasura raged ahead, tossing the high mountains with his horns as his terrible bellowing filled the sky. The earth began to disintegrate under his weight and, lashed by his tail, the seas overflowed. Pierced by his horns the clouds broke into fragments and mountains trembled and collapsed on the earth.

When the Devi saw Mahishasura charging towards her she called all the powers that the devas had given her and assumed her most terrible form. Now raged a battle between the two of them which was so frightening in its intensity that even the devas looking down from the skies shut their eyes. As swift as wind, Durga threw her noose over the buffalo demon's head, but as soon as he was bound Mahishasura quit his buffalo form and became a lion. Then as soon as the Devi cut off his head he made himself a man with a sword. The Devi with lightning speed cut off his head but Mahishasura became a giant elephant. With his huge trunk, the elephant attacked the Devi's lion but as he was dragging him away, she beheaded him with her sword. Then once more, Mahishasura resumed his buffalo form and began to shake the three worlds with his rage. The Devi too was filled with fury and her eyes turned red with anger. She gave a great leap filling the sky, landed on the asura pressing his neck down with her foot and impaled him with her spear. Giving a great howl of pain Mahishasura became half asura and half buffalo as he fought to free himself. The goddess lifted her great sword and with one mighty blow cut off his head. As soon as he was killed, Mahishasura's entire army of asuras too perished with a collective sigh.

The host of devas and all the sages bowed before the Devi as the gandharvas sang and the apsaras danced. One by one, the devas came forward to sing their words of gratitude and to praise the victorious goddess. They worshipped her with flowers from the divine garden Nandan, anointed her with sacred unguents and lit incense.

'O Devi, we bow before you, who are yourself good fortune in the dwellings of the virtuous and ill-fortune in those of the vicious; intelligence in the hearts of the learned; faith in the hearts of the good; and modesty in the hearts of the high-born. May you protect the universe.'

The Devi is called upon again and again to save the devas from the asuras. In this legend from Devimahatmyam, goddess Parvati, the consort of Shiva, assumes the form of Chandika—a goddess who emerges from her own body—to kill two asuras, Sumbha and Nisumbha. Various names are given to the Devi as she battles with the demons and the famous hymn to Aparajita, or hymn to the unvanquished, forms a part of this poem.

'I meditate on the incomparable Mahasaraswati who holds in her lotus-like hands bell, trident, plough, conch, mace, bow and arrow; who is radiant like the moon shining at the fringe of a cloud; who is the destroyer of Sumbha and other asuras; who issued forth from Parvati's body.'

Sumbha and Nisumbha were two giant asuras who right from childhood wanted to be rulers of the three worlds. They decided to do many years of severe penance and even though they were young boys they set out with a firm resolution on their ambitious path. For ten thousand years they sat without food or water till Shiva finally appeared and granted them a boon that their strength and wealth would be greater than that of the devas. As soon as this was said, the two brothers declared war upon Indra's kingdom. Bold and arrogant with their new-found powers, the two asuras soon reduced the devas to slaves. They took over all the sacrifices made to the various devas who quietly went away from heaven and began to live as beggars on earth.

After surviving for a while in this wretched state, they remembered the promise the Devi had made to them. 'She had granted us the boon: "Whenever in calamites you think of me, that very moment I will put an end to all your miseries."' Gathering together their feeble remaining strength they made their way back to heaven and began to pray to Devi.

'Salutation to the Devi, to the Mahadevi. Salutation always to her who is ever auspicious. Salutation to her who is the primordial cause and embodiment of all that is good and benign. To thee we offer our humble obeisance,' sang the devas. As they sat on the banks of the river Ganga praying, Parvati came to bathe in the river. She listened for a while to the songs of prayer and then asked, 'Who is praised by you here?' As she said these words a goddess sprang from her and replied, 'This hymn is addressed to me by the assembled devas who have been vanquished by the two asuras Sumbha and Nisumbha.' The goddess who had emerged from Parvati shone before the devas, assuring them of victory over the asuras. Then she went away to the Himalayas where she began to live in a splendid garden she created.

One day Chanda and Munda, two powerful asuras who served the asura king Sumbha, saw the beautiful goddess alone in the forest. They were astounded by her beauty and raced back to their king to tell him about her. 'O King, a certain woman, most unsurpassingly beautiful, dwells there shedding lustre on Mount Himalaya. Such supreme beauty was never seen by anyone anywhere. Ascertain who that goddess is and take possession of her, O lord of the asuras.' By then Sumbha had captured all the precious jewels in the world. Airavata, the gem among elephants, was his after he stole it from Indra along with the heavenly Parijata tree. Brahma's chariot yoked with swans was also his now and so was the gold-showering umbrella of Varuna. The rare horse Ucchaishravas which emerged during the churning of the milk-ocean too was his. Sumbha, who possessed all this wealth, now wondered why this jewel of a woman was not his. He sent a messenger, Sugriva, to the Devi asking her to quickly come to him. Sugriva found the Devi in a garden on a mountain peak and gave her the message Sumbha had sent. 'O beautiful lady, whatever other rare objects there existed among the devas, gandharvas and nagas are with me.

'We look upon you, O Devi, as the jewel of womankind in the world. Come to me, since we are amongst those who enjoy the best objects.

'Wealth, great beyond compare, you will get by marrying me. Think over this in your mind and become my life.'

The Devi heard the messenger patiently and then she said in a gentle voice, 'You have spoken the truth. Sumbha is indeed the lord of the three worlds and so is Nisumbha. But I made a foolish promise to myself in my youth that I will only marry he who conquers me in battle. I shall only take for my husband the man who removes my pride and is my match in strength. So let the great Sumbha or Nisumbha defeat me here and take my hand in marriage.'

The messenger was aghast. How dare she, a mere woman, challenge his master, the king of the three worlds? He rushed back to relate her words to Sumbha. The king of asuras roared with anger and ordered his general Dhumralochana to go at once and fetch the proud Devi by force. 'Drag that shrew by her hair. Slay anyone who stands up as her saviour, be it a god, yaksha or gandharva,' he thundered. Accompanied by sixty thousand asuras, the general rushed to the mountain peak where the Devi stood. 'Come to my lord, proud woman. If you do not then I will drag you there by your hair.' The Devi stood still and smiled. 'You have been sent by the lord of asuras. You are so mighty yourself with this vast army. What can I do if you take me by force?' she said. Dhumralochana rushed towards her and as he approached her, the Devi uttered a contemptuous sigh of 'hum' reducing the giant asura to a pile of ashes. When Sumbha heard this news, trembling with rage, he commanded his two chief generals to go and fetch the Devi. 'Bind her, let the asuras strike her, wound her. And then bring that shrew here at once,' he roared.

Chanda and Munda marched towards the mountains with a vast army. They saw the Devi on a golden peak seated upon her lion smiling gently. The asuras charged at her with their bows arched and shining swords. The Devi saw them coming towards her and suddenly her skin turned dark with rage. Out of her forehead, fierce and dark with a frowning brow, there suddenly emerged Kali. The terrible goddess glowing with rage was armed with a noose and a gleaming sword. In her hand she held a skull-topped staff decorated with a garland of skulls and from her gaping mouth her tongue lolled out. Crying out with a bloodthirsty roar which filled the sky, the furious goddess began to devour the asuras. Chanda and Munda rushed forward to engage her in battle, but before they could do so, the dark goddess mounted her lion, seized Chanda by his hair and cut his head off with her sword. Then she struck at Munda severing his head in one stroke. 'From now on you shall be called Chamunda for you have destroyed Chanda and Munda so fearlessly,' said the Devi.

Sumbha, raging with fury, now prepared to go into battle himself along with an army of a hundred crore giant asuras. When the gods saw this sea of asuras snaking towards the mountains they knew they had to help the goddess in her encounter with Sumbha and Nisumbha. So out of each of their bodies emerged a 'shakti' goddess endowed with the same strength and power. From Brahma came Brahmani, riding a chariot drawn by swans. She carried a rosary and a kamandal of water which she would sprinkle to make the

asuras inert. From Shiva came Maheshvari adorned with
a digit of the moon and garland of snakes. She was seated
on a bull and held a shimmering trident in her hand. The
shakti of Vishnu, Vaishnavi, came riding on the celestial
bird holding a conch, discus, sword and bow in her hands.
Many other gods too sent their shaktis to the battlefield
and each of these was armed with a formidable weapon.

Then Devi Chandika sent a final warning to the king
of asuras. Since she chose Shiva to be her ambassador she
became known from then on as Shivaduti. 'Tell the two
arrogant asuras to go and live in the nether world and let
the devas rule again. If through pride they are anxious to
battle, come on then. Let my jackals be satiated with their
flesh.'

The king of asuras heard this challenge and stormed
ahead, mad with rage. He hurled arrows, spears, javelins and
axes at her. The Devi calmly faced him with a full-drawn
bow. Then with a light touch she let fly a huge arrow which
shot all his weapons to pieces. Kali pierced the enemies
with her spear, Brahmani sprinkled water which left them
bereft of valour, an angry Maheshvari slew the asuras with
her trident and Vaishnavi threw her discus, cutting them
into pieces. The other shaktis too created havoc.

When the great asura Raktabija saw his army being
vanquished by these enraged shaktis sent by the gods, he
strode forward to join the battle. This asura had a boon that
whenever a drop of blood fell from his body on the ground,
an asura of his stature would rise from that very spot. As
they fought, blood flowed from his body and a whole new
army of asuras rose up at once to battle the Devi and the

shaktis. Soon the entire world was filled with giant asuras and the devas were filled with alarm. Seeing the devas dejected Chandika laughed and said to Kali, 'O Chamunda open your mouth wide and drink this blood that flows from the asura.' So as the Devi showered the giant with arrows, spears and darts, Chamunda went on drinking his blood without letting a drop fall on the ground.

Sumbha, enraged on seeing his great army slaughtered, rushed to slay Chandika. Then began a battle between Sumbha and Nisumbha and the great Devi. Thunderbolts struck like arrows of fire and the sky was filled with war cries as they roared. Nisumbha tried to strike the Devi's lion with his sword but she quickly cut him into pieces. When Nisumbha fell, Sumbha came out on his chariot, holding an array of weapons in his eight arms. The goddess now blew her conch and began pulling at her bow string to make a deafening sound. Her lion roared too as the Devi enlarging her palms struck the sky with an ominous shrill cry of laughter. 'Victory to thee, O Devi!' cried the devas as they watched the terrible battle. The three worlds shook with their war cries as Devi split the arrows shot by Sumbha and he too retaliated by cutting her arrows down. Brahmani, Maheshvari, Vaishnavi and the other shaktis too jumped into the battlefield once more to slay the asuras. With his brother slain and his army slaughtered, Sumbha's rage knew no bounds. 'O Durga,' he shouted with anger, 'You who are so puffed up with pride, you are so haughty yet you resort to help from others when you fight.' When the Devi heard his voice she stood still and faced him. 'I am all alone in the world here. Who else is there beside me? See, O vile one, these goddesses, who are but my own powers, entering into my ownself.' Then one by one all the shaktis were absorbed in the body of the Devi. 'The numerous forms which I projected by my power here have been withdrawn by me, and now I stand alone. Now ready yourself for the final battle.'

Then, as the devas watched, began a terrible battle which lasted for a long time. Sumbha brought out all the divine weapons in his possession but the Devi destroyed them all. After carrying on a fierce fight which rose like a whirlwind of fury into the sky, the Devi lifted him up, whirled him around and flung him down. Then she plunged her spear into his heart and he fell lifeless on the ground, shaking the entire earth and flooding the seas. As soon as the evil asura was slain the universe became calm and peaceful. The sky became clear once more and the dark storm clouds turned tranquil. The rivers kept within their course and as the devas rejoiced, the sun became brilliant, the sacred fires burnt peacefully. A soothing calm now pervaded the world which had been so rocked by battle cries and the gandharvas sang in praise of the Devi:

'O Devi, be pleased and protect us always from fear of foes, as you have done just now by the slaughter of asuras. And destroy quickly the sins of all worlds and the great calamities which have sprung from evil portents.'

Sati

As Sati, a manifestation of Durga, the goddess is the beloved wife of Shiva. We see her now not as a great warrior but as his faithful, gentle wife Uma, who cannot bear the humiliation of her husband, whom she worships as a god, and gives up her life. Her name Sati has come to mean virtuous and it also describes a wife who commits self-immolation on her husband's funeral pyre. The following legend is from the Bhagavata Purana and there are various other versions of this legend in the Mahabharata and Skanda Purana.

One day Uma was sitting with her husband, Lord Shiva, in their home on Mount Kailash when she saw a convoy of glittering chariots passing by. Each one carried a finely bedecked god and his consort. They passed by in a flurry of golden dust and Uma, curious to know what was happening, stood up to gaze at this magnificent convoy. 'Where are they all going? All these gods and goddesses and even the gandharvas. Look, my lord, how they are all dressed up in fine clothes and jewels. You who knows all must know where they are going, dressed in their finest clothes and jewels?' she asked Shiva who was sitting quietly by her side. At first the great lord was silent, but when Uma asked him over and over again, he told her with great reluctance, 'They are all going to your father's house to take part in a great sacrifice he has organized.'

'But why have we, my lord, not been invited?' she asked, bewildered. Shiva did not answer her though he knew why they had not been invited. The great god Rudra was silent because he knew his answer would hurt Uma. His father-in-law, Daksha, who was Brahma's son, had always disliked him and had been against his marrying his beautiful daughter Uma. 'My virtuous fawn-eyed daughter's hand to be given in marriage to this monkey-eyed god? A man who lives amongst the dead, wears bark and adorns himself with ash?' he had protested. But Brahma had told him to let Uma marry Shiva.

Uma lived happily on Mount Kailash with her husband and was content to always be by his side. Her husband's strange and unusual appearance and seemingly odd behaviour did not worry her because she knew in her heart how great and benevolent he was. She understood this king of mountains, his all-powerful mind, his infinite energy which cast its fiery light all over the world. But her father continued to hate him.

One day when Shiva, Brahma and many other gods were seated at a sacrifice ceremony Daksha entered. All those assembled rose to salute him except his father Brahma and Shiva. Daksha, an arrogant man, was very offended. He looked at Shiva angrily and said to the assembled gods, 'Though unwilling, I gave my daughter to this impure and proud abolisher of rites and demolisher of barriers. He roams about in dreadful cemeteries, attended by hosts of ghosts and sprites, like a mad man, naked with dishevelled hair, wearing a garland of dead men's skulls and ornaments of bones. To this wicked-hearted lord of the infuriate, whose purity has perished, I have, alas, given my virtuous daughter. This monkey-eyed god after having taken the hand of my fawn-eyed daughter has not, even by word, shown suitable respect to me, who he should have risen and saluted.' Shiva sat calmly listening to these insulting words. This made Daksha even more angry and rising to his feet, he cursed Shiva. 'Let this Bhava, lowest of the gods, never receive any portion during a sacrifice along with other gods.' Saying this he stormed out of the assembly.

This was the reason why they had not been invited to the great sacrifice but Shiva did not want to tell Uma this because he knew how fragile her heart was.

Uma grew more agitated as she watched the chariots go past. They were all going to her father's house, everyone in heaven except for her. Why should she stay here when all her sisters and other relatives were gathering in Daksha's house, she thought. She too would go. Her father must have forgotten to call her. When she told Shiva about her plans, he tried to stop her. 'Pray, beloved, do not go to your father's house. You are not wanted there. They will insult you. Please remain here in our mountain home which is so far from everyone,' said the great lord.

'Why should they insult me? My father will be happy to see me. I am his youngest and favourite daughter. He always loved me more than my sisters. I must go. I will go alone, my lord, if you do not wish to accompany me. I know you do not like to leave the mountains,' replied Uma and set out alone for her father's house. She arrived at Daksha's magnificent palace to find all other gods and goddess, demigods and her sisters were happily settled in but there was no one to welcome her. Uma went in search of her father, eager to see him. As she walked down the palace corridors, her sisters and their husbands followed her, laughing and ridiculing Shiva. 'Where is your great lord and master? Enjoying his ganja sleep, covered in ashes? Has he given you any jewels as yet or just a garland of skulls? Where are your ghosts?' Uma ignored them and ran to her father. She touched his feet and said, 'I rushed here, Father, as soon as I heard about the sacrifice. But why have you not called my lord Shiva to this great sacrifice? How can this ceremony take place without the supreme god?' she asked with tears in her eyes. Daksha flared up at once when he heard Shiva's name. 'Who has ever regarded Shiva as a god, leave alone the supreme god? Only you, my foolish child, were keen to marry him, this lowly creature who lives amongst the dead. You have lowered your dignity and my honour by becoming his wife. I do not want to insult my honoured guests with his lowly presence. I will never have his dark presence in my house,' said Daksha. Uma was stunned by her father's cruel words. She could not bear to hear him speak about Shiva, her beloved husband, in this demeaning way. Her heart was filled with pain. Bowing her head, she closed her eyes and thought of her husband. 'Lord, among all beings you are supreme in power because of your qualities. You are invincible, unapproachable because of your energy, fame and glory. Illustrious one, sinless one, great sorrow and trembling have come upon me because you have been denied your share in this sacrifice.' Saying this she gave up her life.

When Shiva heard that Uma had died he was filled with rage. His eyes blazed with anger and fire as he cursed Daksha. The lord of lords gathered his formidable powers and from the lock of his hair arose a gigantic thousand-armed demon. His head touched the skies and his feet dug into the nether world. His gaping mouth was filled with monstrous teeth dripping with blood. As this hideous giant named Virbhadra strode out, heaven and earth trembled with fear. Shiva commanded him to destroy Daksha and his sacrifice which had cost Uma her life. His fierce rage blazing like a forest fire, Shiva now charged down from Mount Kailash in a cloud of thunder and black smoke to destroy everything in his path. Reaching Daksha's palace with an army of giants, ghosts and sprites, he took hold of Daksha and tore his head from his body. The gods ran about trying desperately to escape Shiva's wrath and the sacrifice converting itself into a deer tried to flee but Shiva's arrow caught it.

When Shiva saw Sati's body lying dead on the ground he went mad with grief. His howls of anger and pain filled the sky till the mountains rocked and weeping he picked up Sati's body. His grief had turned him insane and he began walking with her body to the four corners of the earth. Blind with anger and sorrow, he danced in a frenzy of madness, scattering Sati's limbs and her ornaments all over the land. Wherever the various parts of the goddess's body fell, a shrine was built in her memory. As Shiva roamed the earth, his rage showing no signs of abating, the gods grew frightened. 'He will destroy us all if we do not stop him. But who will face his wrath? His burning gaze will turn him to ashes at once,' they said, their voices quivering with fear. Finally they went to Brahma and told him what had happened at Daksha's sacrifice ceremony. The lord of creation who had known what was to happen had not accepted Daksha's invitation. 'Go to Mount Kailash and ask for Shiva's forgiveness. He who is quick to anger is also easy to please. Recognize his true goodness. Know him as the supreme god and offer him your sincere prayers and share of sacrifice. This alone can help you stem his torrent of rage.' The gods rushed to Kailash where they found the great lord still immersed in deep sorrow, mourning for Sati. They fell at his feet crying for his forgiveness. In his greatness Shiva forgave them and even restored Daksha's head with a goat's head.

Then Vishnu spoke to him, 'O Shiva, recover your senses and listen to me. You will certainly find Sati, since you are as inseparable from her as cold from water, heat from fire, smell from earth or radiance from the sun.' As Shiva sat alone in his mountain home, Uma appeared to him bathed in a golden light. 'O Mahadeva, lord of my soul, in whatever state I exist I shall never be separated from my lord, and now I have been born as Parvati, daughter of Himavat, in order to become again thy wife. Therefore no longer grieve on account of our separation.' Saying this she disappeared. Shiva remained still in deep meditation, calm and at peace, knowing Sati would become his wife again in her next life as Parvati.

Parvati was born in the home of the mountain god Himavat. When she was a young girl a sage came to their home and told her that she would one day marry an ascetic whose body was covered with ash. Parvati knew he meant that she was destined for Lord Shiva.

She soon grew up into a woman with such flawless beauty and ethereal grace that even the gods fell in love with her. Confident and somewhat proud, she declared that she would only have Shiva as her husband. A heavenly voice spoke to her, telling her she would have to practise severe austerities to gain Shiva as her husband but Parvati, proud of her great beauty and youth, just laughed disdainfully. 'How can he not be my husband? He who has mourned for me so long—how can he not take me as a wife now that I am redolent of life? We who have been predestined from our first being to be husband and wife—how can any distance exist between us,' she said, confident that Shiva would marry her as soon as he set eyes on her lovely face. She continued to play on the mountains, dance and sing with her friends, quite secure about her future as Shiva's wife. But soon her hopes were shattered. Shiva, she learnt to her dismay, was totally immersed in deep meditation and none could even approach the peak where he sat. Parvati asked the god of love, Kama, to help her gain Shiva's attention. 'Once he opens his eyes and sees me he is sure to fall in love with me. If you help me with your love darts then surely I will not fail to win his heart. I am already his, chosen by destiny. If he will only look at my face just once.'

Kamadeva agreed to help the lovely Parvati and began to work his magic at once. A soothing, warm breeze began to blow and bees hummed a love song. Buds blossomed into flowers filled with sweet nectar and their fragrance filled the lonely mountain meadows where Shiva sat in meditation. At first nothing could break his concentration. Kamadeva's love magic began to cast its spell but the great god was not disturbed by its heady fragrance. Then Kamadeva picked up his bow and shot an arrow of love. There was such silence that it seemed as if the world had stopped moving. Slowly with intense anger Shiva opened his third eye to see who dared to disturb his meditation. His gaze, shimmering with fire, fell on Kamadeva who was right in his line of vision and the god of love was burnt to ashes in this fleeting ray of light. Without a glance at

Parvati, Shiva then moved away to a higher place in the mountains where he could not be disturbed again.

Now Parvati, unhappy and distraught, remembered those heavenly words. 'Why did I, in my foolishness ignore those wise words. Now I shall punish this body of mine which was once so proud of its beauty.' And choosing a remote place in the mountains, she began to perform severe penance which lasted for many years. She, a young girl, outdid most great sages in practising austerities by living only on air and leaves. Soon she gave up eating leaves too and thus became known as Aparna, or one who shuns leaves.

When, summer came and the sun blazed on her, she lit four fires facing north, south, east and west and sat down in the centre of this burning circle with her eyes on the sun. In winter she sat in the ice-cold waters of a mountain lake, her delicate body turning blue with cold. Unaware of hunger or thirst, heat or cold, she meditated day and night on Shiva's memory, crying for his embrace. Her body became frail and the lustre of her golden skin faded like a fallen leaf.

One day an ascetic arrived at the place of her meditation and asked about her welfare. 'Why do you want to marry a god who has no riches, no palace of gold, no heavenly chariots? You, who are so beautiful, should not lack any suitors. Why should you, a jewel, throw yourself away? Shiva's face and body are terrible to behold and his habits are uncivilized and inauspicious. He is a beggar who lives in the land of dead bodies. O lovely, lotus-eyed maiden, pray do not marry such a distasteful character, I beg of you.'

At first Parvati ignored his words but then as he persisted in dissuading her from marrying Shiva, she rose angrily to reply. 'Who are you to speak thus of my lord? He is the core of my being. I belong to him and none else. Only he can claim me as his wife. He who is the lord of gods, on whom the crescent moon shines, who looks like the dark night touched by the light of the moon—my heart belongs to him. I shall marry only him,' she said and shut her eyes. Suddenly the mountain was ablaze with light as Shiva himself appeared before her. Frightened by his sudden presence, Parvati tried to move away but Shiva held her in his arms as the gods showered their blessings on them. Once more Shiva and Parvati were united as they were meant to be.

Lakshmi

Lakshmi is one of the most sought after goddesses in Hindu mythology. Shri or Lakshmi, as depicted in the sacred texts, is the goddess of wealth and fortune, royal power and beauty. 'Shri-sukta', a hymn from the Rig Veda in praise of Lakshmi, gives a detailed description of her many virtues. She is invoked to bring fame and prosperity. She is bountiful and bestows upon her worshippers gold, cattle, horses and abundant food.

The hymn, one of the earliest dedicated to the goddess, associates many symbols with her. She is described as a beautiful goddess as lustrous as the moon who wears ornaments of gold and silver. Lakshmi is depicted seated on a lotus, her skin is the colour of a lotus in bloom and she wears a garland of lotuses too. Lakshmi, in fact, is often called Padma. Very often the goddess is shown in her Gajalakshmi image with elephants on either side showering her with water from their trunks.

Her other well-known forms are Rajyalakshmi where she is the companion of every ruler, a royal deity who protects the king as long as he remains true to the path of virtue but abandons him if he forsakes his princely duties and becomes an unworthy ruler. She is also known as Jayalakshmi, the goddess of victory, who changes sides as and when she wishes. Another popular form of the goddess is Grihalakshmi, the good, virtuous wife who takes care of her household with devotion.

She is also Bhagyalakshmi, the goddess of one's destiny and good fortune as well as Yasholakshmi, the goddess of fame. Her name is associated with all womanly virtues in Hindu tradition and newly-wed brides are often called 'Lakshmi' in the hope that she will bring good fortune to the household.

Lakshmi is worshipped throughout the year in a variety of festivals in cities as well as in villages. The most important festival associated with her is Deepavali when she is invoked to bring wealth and prosperity to the homes of her worshippers. Many Lakshmi devotees stay awake all night with the doors and windows of their houses open so that Lakshmi can enter and bless them with her presence. Since the goddess brings good fortune, on this day merchants and traders worship their account books too. A festival in rural Bengal celebrates the victory of Lakshmi, the good sister, over her sister Alakshmi, who is supposed to bring misfortune, poverty and hunger. A straw image is created and then destroyed with great fanfare and an image of Lakshmi is installed in her place.

By the late epic period (400 AD) Lakshmi became associated with Vishnu as his devoted wife. In Vishnu Purana we read, 'Shri, the bride of Vishnu, the mother of the world, is eternal, imperishable. As he is all-pervading so she is omnipresent. Vishnu is meaning, she is speech; he is polity, she's prudence; he understanding, and she intellect; he righteousness, and she devotion. In a word Vishnu is all that is called male and Lakshmi all that is termed female; there is nothing else than they.'

Though Lakshmi, being the goddess of fortune, is sometimes called fickle by devotees when she abandons them to poverty, her loyalty to Vishnu, her lord, is so steadfast that she is born as his wife in his various incarnations. The Vishnu Purana gives an account of her various names as the consort of Vishnu. 'As the lord of the worlds, the god of gods, Janardana descends amongst mankind in various shapes, and so does his consort Shri. Thus, when Hari was born as a dwarf, the son of Aditi, Lakshmi appeared from the lotus as Padma, or Kamala; when he was born as Rama (Parashurama) of the race of Bhrigu, she was Dharini; when he was Raghava (Ramachandra), she was Sita; when he was Krishna, she was Rukmini. In the other descents of

Vishnu she was his associate. If he takes a celestial form, she appears as divine; if he is a mortal, she becomes mortal too, transforming her own person agreeably to whatever character it pleases Vishnu to assume.'

Lakshmi's first meeting with Vishnu is described in the legend of the churning of the ocean, which is given in detail in both the epics—Mahabharata and the Ramayana—as well as in the Vishnu Purana, Bhagavata Purana and Padma Purana. The following story is from the Vishnu Purana.

A sage named Durvaras was travelling when he met a celestial nymph who had a garland of fragrant flowers. The sage requested the maiden to give him the garland which she did at once. The sweet scent of the flowers intoxicated the sage and he began dancing with joy. Just then Indra, the lord of heaven, came by and the sage, in a benevolent mood, presented the celestial garland to him. Indra, unaware of the garland's mystical powers, threw it playfully on his elephant's head. The heady scent excited the elephant so much that he seized the garland with his trunk and cast it away. It flew in the air and fell on the ground. Sage Durvaras, furious at the way Indra had slighted his gift, cursed the lord of heaven. 'Your kingdom will be ruined,' he said. From then on Indra's powers began to wane. He begged the sage to forgive him but the curse would not leave him. Soon all the gods in heaven too began to lose their powers one by one and became afraid that the asuras would take over heaven. Feeble and fearful, they fled to Brahma for help. The lord of creation said he could not help them but Vishnu could perhaps find a way out of the crisis. The gods hastily went to Vishnu and pleaded for his help. Vishnu heard their plea and then told them what to do: 'Your strength shall be restored, only accomplish what I now command. Unite yourselves in peaceful combination with these your foes; collect all plants and herbs of diverse kinds from every quarter; cast them into the sea of milk, take Mandara the mountain for a churning stick, and Vasuki the serpent for a rope, together churn the ocean to produce the source of all strength and immortality. Then reckon on mine aid. I will take care. Your foes shall share your toil but not partake in its reward or drink the immortal draught.'

So the gods made friends with their enemies and started out at once to search for the precious herbs as Vishnu had told them to. The mountain Mandara agreed to help them and so did the serpent god Vasuki. 'But who will bear our combined weight?' they asked. Then Vishnu himself came forward in his gigantic tortoise form and on this pivot the churning began with great fanfare. The gods formed a line on one side while the demons took the other end of Vasuki and together they churned the ocean of milk with all their might. But to their shock the first gift that the ocean gave was a deadly poison. Shiva quickly swallowed it, thus saving the world from destruction. The poison remained in his throat, giving it a blue tinge and he was named Neelkanth, or the one with the blue throat, hereafter.

As the gods and the demons twisted and turned the serpent, many precious gifts arose from the ocean. Surabhi, the eternal fountain of milk; Varuni, the god of wine; Parijata, the tree of paradise, which filled the world with its fragrant blossoms; Ucchaishravas, the unique horse;

Airavata, the divine elephant; and a bevy of beautiful apsaras emerged from the ocean along with many other precious gifts. Then emerged the goddess Lakshmi, seated on a lotus.

When she appeared the gods were enraptured and the heavenly choristers, the gandharvas, sang her praise while the apsaras danced around her. Ganga, the sacred river, followed her while heavenly elephants poured water over her. The ocean presented her with a garland of never-fading lotuses. Adorned with ornaments which the gods had presented to her, she rose from the ocean of milk, dazzling all who beheld her.

A poem from Ramayana (translated by Griffith) describes her with these lyrical words:

When many a year had fled,
Up floated, on her lotus bed,
A maiden fair, and tender eyed
In the young flush of beauty's pride.
She shone with pearl and golden sheen,
And seals of glory stamped her queen.
On each round arm glowed many a gem,
On her smooth brows a diadem.
Rolling in waves beneath her crown
The glory of her hair rolled down
Pearls on her neck of price untold,
The lady shone like burnished gold.
Queen of the gods, she leapt to land,
A lotus in her perfect hand,
And fondly of the lotus sprung,

To lotus-bearing Vishnu clung,
Her, gods above and men below
As Beauty's Queen and Fortune know.

When Dhanvantari finally emerged from the ocean, carrying the pot of nectar, both the gods and the demons rushed to take it from his hands. Before the gods could reach him, the asuras, who were faster and more aggressive, carried away the vessel of amrita. The gods once more beseeched Lord Vishnu to come to their aid. Vishnu then took the form of a beautiful celestial maiden called Mohini. The demons had started quarrelling about who should drink the ambrosia first, and it was at this moment that Mohini appeared before them. The demons, overcome with passion, forgot their draught of immortality and rushed towards her. She offered to distribute the amrita equally amongst the demons. Totally bewitched by her beauty, they handed over the precious nectar to her. Mohini distributed the nectar to the gods and disappeared at once. Pandemonium broke loose but it was too late for the demons to do anything. They had been tricked out of immortality by Vishnu's maya. The lord of preservation was rewarded for his effort with Lakshmi who became his consort forever.

The following popular legend tells the story of how Rajyalakshmi takes sides according to her wishes.

Prahlad, the son of a demon named Virochana, was a good but meek king. Lakshmi, impressed with his princely virtues, decided to come and stay by his side but this made the gods uneasy. They asked Indra to request her to return to heaven. Lakshmi could not refuse him since he was the lord of heaven. As soon as she left Prahlad, his fortunes began to wane and all his royal might slipped away from him. He was soon reduced to a weak and impoverished ruler with no one to help him. Prahlad's son Bali realized why Lakshmi had left his father. 'The gods took her away because you were a meek, gentle and quiet king. They felt you did not deserve to have the goddess by your side. A king should be brave and valiant. He should go out to conquer the world. The goddess Lakshmi favours only those kings who are brave and valiant. I will show the goddess what a great king I can be and then surely she will return to us,' said Bali, who though virtuous like his father was also a formidable warrior. Soon, with a powerful combination of austere devotions and brave conquests, he had captured all the three worlds.

Once again the gods asked Vishnu to come to their rescue and save their heaven from Bali. Lord Vishnu then appeared before Bali, who was reigning in Indra's heaven, in the form of a dwarf Brahman, or his Vamana avatar. 'Welcome, O Brahman. What can we do for thee? Ask for me whatever thou desirest,' said the virtuous demon king. Vishnu, as the dwarf, then said to Bali, 'I ask from thee a small portion of ground, three paces measured step by step. I desire no more of thee. A wise man incurs no sin when he asks for as much as he needs.' Bali, though surprised at this small request, agreed at once. Then Vishnu assumed his cosmic form and took his first step which covered the entire earth. With his second step he reached across from one side of the heaven to the other. With his third step he could reach into the nether world but he stopped. 'Where shall I place my third step, O King,' he asked. Bali, who knew now that it was Vishnu who stood before him, bowed his head and said, 'Place thy foot upon my head. I fear not the nether world as much as a bad name,' and went away to live in the underworld. Indra regained his heaven and Lord Vishnu once more had goddess Lakshmi by his side.

The Devi Bhagavata Purana gives an account of the goddess Lakshmi being turned into a mare by Vishnu's curse.

Once due to some reason known only to Vishnu, he cursed his wife Lakshmi and turned her into a mare.

Though she was saddened by this she obeyed her husband and went away to live as a mare in the underworld. She chose a quiet, verdant forest where the two rivers Yamuna and Tamasa met and sat down to meditate. The goddess whose beauty glowed like the moon was content to be a mare since this was Vishnu's wish and she knew that he must have some reason to make her live in this form.

She began to meditate not on Vishnu but on Shiva, the god of the mountains. With a single-minded concentration she thought only of Shiva, the god with five faces and ten arms, whose glory was enhanced by his beautiful consort Parvati, whose pale body shone like moonlight, whose throat was marked blue with the poison he had swallowed, whose three eyes knew the three worlds, who wore an elephant's hide around his shoulders. She thought of the god who wore a garland of skulls around his neck and a gleaming serpent on his body. Days went by and seasons changed the forest from a canopy of green to a leafless, dry hill. Thousands of years passed as the goddess prayed to Shiva.

Then, pleased with her devotion, Shiva appeared before her one day. Riding his bull, he came to the sacred confluence of rivers with Parvati by his side. They beheld the goddess in her mare form and Shiva spoke to her. 'Why are you here, gentle woman? What need do you have to meditate? You are the beloved wife of Vishnu—the lord of the universe, the one who grants everyone's wishes. Why do you leave such a supreme god and pray to me? The entire world prays to your husband who is the most benevolent of all gods and yet you think of me. Why is it so? A good wife should only serve her husband and your husband is the great god Vishnu. You must pray to him and not me,' said Shiva.

Lakshmi heard the words spoken by Shiva quietly and then she bowed to him and replied, 'O Lord! You who are so kind to your worshippers, I wish to tell you that my husband has cursed me. That is the reason I sit here on the banks of the rivers Yamuna and Tamasa in the form of a mare. That is why I pray to you day and night. Please release me from this curse. My lord said to me, "You shall return to me only after you have borne a son." Tell me, the lord with three eyes whose glance takes in the three worlds in one sweep, tell me how shall I have a son when my husband is not with me? When I am not in his care, how can I give birth to a child?' When Shiva did not reply to her she cast her eyes down and said, 'If you are pleased with my devotion then pray grant me a boon. There is no difference between my lord Vishnu and you. I have known this supreme truth ever since I have been with my lord. What you are, so is he and what he is, is the same as you. This is what is known to me and that is why I meditated and prayed to you.'

Then Shiva spoke. 'You are right. There is no difference between Vishnu and me. But how do you know this secret? Great sages have failed to come to this conclusion. How did you know this as the truth when it has confused so many of our devotees who see us as different forms? Tell me,' asked Shiva smiling at the goddess who had greatly pleased him.

Lakshmi replied, 'One day I was watching Vishnu who was in deep meditation. He sat alone totally detached from the world, his mind resting on a divine being. I did not disturb him but when he had finished his meditation and opened his eyes, his face gleaming with joy, I dared to ask him this question: "Lord, you who are a supreme god, above all other gods, it was you whom I chose when I rose out of the milk of ocean. I saw all the gods assembled there but you stood above them all. I realized then at once that you are the greatest of them all and that is why I chose to belong to you. But then who are you praying to? Who is above you in this world, my lord?" Vishnu, the lord of preservation replied thus to me, "Listen and I will tell you. With all my heart and mind I was meditating upon the image of Shiva, he who is so great yet so easily pleased. I was meditating upon him as he often meditates upon me. He is as dear to me as I am to him. We are bound together by a great love and there is no difference between us. Those who pray to me also pray to him and those who pray to me and do not show reverence to him shall never attain heaven." After Vishnu, my lord, had spoken these words to me I knew that you and he are the same so I prayed to you. I know that only you can lift the curse that is upon me and help me attain my husband once more,' said the goddess with tears in her eyes.

Shiva then placed his hand upon her head and spoke to her in a gentle tone. 'Be patient. Your wish will be granted. I am greatly pleased by your devotion and you will be reunited with your husband soon. When he hears my voice in his head, he will come here in the shape of a horse. You will be the proud mother of a beautiful son just as he had wished. The entire world will bow before this child and he shall rule the earth one day. After your son is born you shall return to Vaikunth once more with your husband and live there happily as his beloved wife.'

As Shiva had predicted, Vishnu came to meet Lakshmi in the form of a stallion. A son named Ekvir was born to her, who later became famous for his noble deeds.

One aspect of Lakshmi is Shri—fortune or prosperity. Another is Bhu or Prithivi—earth—a name she receives from Prithu, son of Vena and the first king to have been installed on earth.

According to the Vishnu Purana, the sages made Vena king of the earth, but he was wicked and banned rituals and worship. So the sages beat him to death. But the world still needed a king, so the sages rubbed the thigh of Vena's corpse, and his sins came out as the evil Nishadas. Then they rubbed his right arm and out came Prithu, who was crowned king of the universe.

Meanwhile, famine was ravaging the land. So the people approached Prithu and asked him for the plants that the earth refused to yield. Prithu threatened the earth, who took the form of a cow. Prithu 'milked' her, making her yield numerous varieties of grain and vegetables. The earth is described as a cow and the milking is symbolic of the extraction of agriculture and prosperity. Because he granted her life, Prithu is the earth's father; hence the name Prithivi.

The word Prithivi itself means broad, signifying the wide world or the earth. She is the mother of all beings and is invoked along with the sky. There are three earths corresponding to the three heavens. Our earth is Bhumi or Bhu or Prithivi.

Saraswati

Saraswati is one of the few important goddesses who has retained her glory from the Vedic age to the Puranic age and is still worshipped in many parts of India. At first she was known only as a river goddess and was associated in the Vedas with the mighty river Saraswati. Her name literally means 'the watery one'. There are frequent mentions in the Vedas that important rituals were performed on the banks of the river Saraswati. In the Rig Veda she is said to heal the god Indra along with the twin gods Asvins. During the later periods, Saraswati's connection with the river decreases and she begins to be invoked as Vagdevi—the goddess of speech. Her other names too describe her as a speech deity and she is known as Jihvagravasini (dwelling in the front of the tongue), Kavijihvagravasini (she who dwells on the tongues of poets) and Mahavani (possessing great speech). Gradually Saraswati's benevolent powers began to encompass poetry, music and all creative arts and to this day this is how she is worshipped in many parts of India.

A hymn from the Rig Veda praises Saraswati with these words: 'Ye, opulent waters, command riches; ye possess excellent power and immortality; ye are the mistress of wealth and progeny; may Saraswati bestow this vitality on her worshipper' (Rig Veda vi. 52–6).

Saraswati is considered the muse of poets, artists and musicians and she is invoked by them whenever artistic excellence is desired. Even the gandharvas, the celestial singers and dancers, pray to her for inspiration before they sing or dance in the presence of gods. As a residing deity of the arts and learning, the goddess of wisdom, the mother of the Vedas, the inventor of the Devnagri script, prayers to Saraswati are offered every morning in schools and colleges in many parts of India.

The image of Saraswati in art is always serene and her colours are predominantly white and yellow, sometimes with a touch of blue to remind the devotee of her earlier image as a river goddess. She has four arms and holds a book, a veena, a rosary, and a water pot. The book is a

symbol of learning, the veena associates her with musical
arts while the rosary or string of pearls and the water pot
are symbols of religious rites. Sometimes the goddess
is depicted with two arms, seated on a lotus, playing the
veena. Her mount is usually a pure white swan, its image
matching the goddess in purity and serenity.

Saraswati is worshipped in the month of Magh
(January) with a simple ritual, unlike her sister goddesses.
Sometimes instead of an idol of the goddess, a book or
a pen is worshipped, mostly by students. On the day of
Saraswati Puja, students are given a day off from learning
and not allowed to write or read. The last watch of the
night is considered especially sacred to Saraswati according
to the Laws of Manu.

'Let the housekeeper awake in time sacred to Brahmi
[one of her names, the feminine form of Brahma] goddess
of speech, reflect on virtue and virtuous employments, and
on the whole meaning and very essence of the Vedas.'

Saraswati, according to the Devi Bhagavata Purana, is
one of the five dynamic female forces which emerged
from the supreme spirit: 'Durga, Lakshmi, Saraswati,
Savitri and Radha, these five goddesses are the spirit of
Prakriti and the entire universal force emerges from these
five. Listen Narada, in the beginning of creation Brahma
divided himself into two—Prakriti and Purush. All the
virtuous qualities of the great Creator are contained in
these two forms.'

Krishna, the first complete Purush, in order to carry forth the act of creation, divides himself into male and female. The female form then further divides herself into five and Saras is one of these goddesses. Each goddess has a specific power and Saraswati is endowed with the creative force of knowledge and learning.

Saraswati's origin differs in the various Puranas. In the Matsya Purana, Saraswati is said to have been born from Brahma when, desiring to create the world, he went into deep meditation.

Enraptured by his female self, who was Saraswati, Brahma desired her, mated with her and created the demigod Manu. In a folk myth based on this legend, Saraswati tried to escape her father's amorous attentions by running away. But she was not able to hide as he grew a head in whichever direction she fled. Some myths forgive Brahma this sin of incest by stating that he was fooled by Madana, the god of love, who was later burnt to ashes because of this misdeed. There are many other versions of this popular tale.

Saraswati's earlier origin can be seen in the Vamana Purana where her identity as the Vedic river goddess is retained and she is said to be the presiding deity of thunder, clouds and rain.

Most puranic texts associate Saraswati with Brahma the Creator right from the time he began to form the universe. The Brahmavaivarta Purana says: 'When Brahma had fashioned all this universe, he placed his seed in Savitri [one of the names of Saraswati in this text] his best wife, as a man full of desire places his seed in a woman full of desire. For a hundred celestial years she held the embryo, which was difficult to bear, and then when she was ready to give birth she bore four enchanting Vedas; the various branches of knowledge such as logic and grammar; the thirty-six celestial Raginis that capture the heart; and the six beautiful Ragas with their various rhythms.'

A verse from the Mahabharata says: 'A voice derived from Brahma entered into the ears of them all; the celestial Saraswati was then produced from the heavens.'

But it is not Brahma who is her husband but Vishnu, according to the Skanda Purana. In this text it is mentioned that she emerged from Vishnu who held her on his tongue. Sometimes she is depicted as being his tongue. Because of her association with Vishnu, many popular myths depict her as a jealous co-wife of Lakshmi which somehow goes against her serene, goddess-of-the-intellect image.

According to the Devi Bhagavata Purana, Saraswati was the wife of Vishnu along with Lakshmi and Ganga. But in later mythology she becomes the consort of Brahma. This legend from the Devi Bhagavata Purana narrates how this came about.

The three lovely goddesses were all wives of Vishnu and lived in Vaikunth. While Lakshmi and Ganga were content and spoke lovingly to each other and to their husband, Saraswati was not happy about sharing the love and affection of her lord Vishnu. She followed the other wives with jealous eyes and soon began to believe that her husband loved Ganga much more than he loved her. Though this thought worried her all the time, she could not bring herself to complain to the lord. But as days went by her jealous heart grew more and more distraught and one day while the three of them were sitting together, she could no longer contain herself and suddenly rose up to accuse Ganga with these angry words: 'You have stolen my husband from me. He who used to have so much love for me, now he only looks at you.' Saying this she turned towards Lord Vishnu who had just entered the room. Her anger making her bolder than ever, Saraswati continued her tirade against Ganga. 'I know that she is the one you love now. Am I not your beloved wife too? Yet you have loving glances only for that one. You wish to see her by your side and not me.'

Vishnu, who loved his three wives equally, and did not wish to interfere in their quarrels, moved away ignoring her harsh words and this enraged Saraswati even more. Turning angrily towards Ganga, she cried, 'Begone from my sight you wretched woman. You are a thief who has stolen my husband's love. He was my lord and you took him from me,' she said over and over again till poor Ganga could bear it no more and begged Vishnu to help her. But the lord of preservation remained calm and detached. His lotus eyes remained shut and his face was as still as a pool of water.

Then Lakshmi who had been sitting quietly, listening to Saraswati as she raged, decided to come to Ganga's rescue. 'Leave her alone. She has done you no harm. Our lord loves us all equally. We three are blessed by his golden, benevolent light which falls impartially on us like the rays of the sun. O sister, I beg of you, leave Ganga alone,' said Lakshmi in her gentle voice. Her sweet words instead of calming Saraswati's anger made her even more furious and the goddess of learning now turned her fiery eyes towards her. 'How dare you take sides? You are my sister you say, yet I can see you love Ganga more than me. Both of you want me to leave so that you can share my husband's love between the two of you instead of three of us. You are supposed to be my loyal sister but I will curse you today. You shall be born on earth as a plant.'

Lakshmi heard Saraswati's harsh words with a bowed head. She did not even lift her eyes to retaliate. She did not curse Saraswati in return though she could do so if she wished. She remained her calm and benevolent self, but her heart was touched by her sister's unhappiness and she moved forward to sooth Saraswati's angry brow. Though Lakshmi did not react to Saraswati's curse, Ganga, when she saw her beloved Lakshmi being berated by Saraswati, could not restrain herself. 'My true sister whom I love so dearly, who has never spoken an unkind word ever. I cannot bear it when this one so crazed with jealousy speaks like this to you. This Saraswati who cursed you will herself turn into a river. She will only flow in the dark crevices of hell where only evil men live,' said Ganga trembling with anger. These words made Saraswati flare up like a haystack on fire. She at once retaliated with another curse. 'You, the one who steals love which belongs to another woman, you with the sly eyes and a bee's sting will also flow in hell and on earth. You will turn into a river where men will wash their sins forever.' While the two goddesses raged with anger, Lakshmi sat in between as placid and calm as a moonbeam.

Then Lord Vishnu decided to put an end to this quarrel, and came into their midst once more, shining like a tower of gold. He called Saraswati to him and put his hand on her head affectionately to cool her temper. The lord of preservation already knew why they were quarrelling and what the outcome would be. 'Beloved wife,' he said addressing the gentle Lakshmi first who sat with her eyes cast down. 'You will live on earth as the sacred plant Tulsi. But that will come later, first you shall descend to earth and live as the river Padmavati.' Then he turned to Ganga, 'You too will descend to the earth and flow as the river Bhagirathi. With your waters pure you will cleanse and release the souls of Bhagirath's kinsmen who are lying in hell.' Then finally the lord of preservation turned to Saraswati who now sat quietly by his side, full of remorse. 'You too will have to accept Ganga's curse and go down to the earth as a river. Later you will be worshipped for your skill in arts and learning.' Then Vishnu looked at Lakshmi once more. 'Only she will return to me. She, who is the embodiment of womanly grace and kindness. She who glows with compassion, who is great and all forgiving. I have immense respect for her because she is full of virtue.' As Ganga and Saraswati bowed their heads, Lakshmi spoke on their behalf. 'We will do as you say as it is our destiny. But when will we be reunited with you? I must know because I cannot exist without you. When will you rescue me from my fate?' said the goddess of compassion and placed her head on Vishnu's lotus feet.

Vishnu heard her plea and smiled at her. He embraced her and said, 'I must keep my word and yet I must be fair to all three. Saraswati, a part of you will remain with me and another part will go to earth and yet another part will go to Brahma and remain with him. Ganga, you will go as I said to release the souls of Bhagirath's kinsmen but before that you will have the honour of living for a while on Shiva's head.' Then with tenderness in his eyes Vishnu looked at Lakshmi. 'You have to suffer the curse as it was ordained. Our separation will be for a thousand years but after that period you will return to me and we shall be together forever.' Saying this, Vishnu left them to carry out their destiny and journey to earth.

Another legend from the Skanda Purana tells us once more about the fiery temper of Saraswati. This time she leaves Brahma in a fit of anger. The story is narrated by Shiva to Parvati. Saraswati is known as Savitri here. A verse in Matsya Purana says she is called by several names, 'Brahma next formed from his immaculate substance a female who is celebrated under the names of Satrupa, Savitri, Saraswati, Gayatri and Brahmani.' Though in this legend from the Skanda Purana Savitri is the goddess Saraswati, Gayatri is another woman who causes a rift between Brahma and Saraswati.

'Listen, O Devi, and I will tell you how Saraswati forsook Brahma and he in consequence espoused Gayatri,' said Shiva to Parvati narrating the story.

Brahma along with Saraswati and many gods and holy sages went to Pushkar where a great sacrifice was being organized to bestow rain on the earth. All the preparations had been made to ensure that the rites and ceremonies went according to what had been prescribed by the gods. Suddenly some of the priests looked around and declared that Saraswati was not there. Brahma was surprised and he hastily sent a priest to call her. 'Tell her to come at once so that the ceremony is not delayed. The auspicious hour must not pass,' said the lord of creation. But when the priest returned he was alone. 'The Devi says she is not yet ready.' Another priest was sent to fetch her with an urgent message but he too came back without the goddess but with a message for the assembled gods. 'Tell them that I have not yet completed my dress nor arranged the household affairs. And moreover Lakshmi, Ganga, Indrani and the wives of other gods have not yet arrived so why should I proceed to the assembly with such unseemly haste?'

The priest then addressed Brahma. 'Saraswati is engaged and will not come; but without a wife what advantage can be derived from these rites?' Brahma, incensed at his wife's conduct commanded Indra, 'Hasten and in obedience to my order bring a wife from wherever you can find one.' Indra left the assembly at once and began to search for a suitable wife for Brahma. As he was walking, wondering where he would find such a woman, he saw a young and beautiful milkmaid, carrying a jar of butter. Her smiling face was glowing and her voice was soft as milk and honey. 'She will do,' he said and seizing her, brought her to Brahma at once. Brahma then addressed the assembly. 'O gods and holy sages, if it seems good unto you I will espouse this Gayatri, and she shall become the mother of the Vedas, and the cause of purity to these worlds.'

The milkmaid now known as Gayatri was arrayed in fine silken garments and bedecked with costly ornaments and led to the bower of the bride. In front of the entire assembly, the lord of creation was married to Gayatri.

At this very moment when the wedding vows were complete, Saraswati, her various chores done, finally arrived at the assembly accompanied by the wives of Vishnu, Shiva and other gods. She was filled with rage when she saw the milkmaid in the bridal bower, glittering with jewels. Overcome with anger, she could not speak for a moment and then angry words rushed from her like a river in flood. 'O Brahma. You have rejected me, your wedded wife, for this milkmaid. Have you no sense of shame to discard me like this? You, who are called the great father of gods and holy sages—how could you commit such a sinful act which will shock all the three worlds? O Lord, how can I show my face to the world now that you have forsaken me? Deserted by my husband, I can no longer call myself a wife.' Brahma heard her angry speech calmly and when she had finished, replied, 'Calm yourself, wife. I did so because the priests informed me that the time for the sacrifice was passing away and that it could not be performed properly unless my wife was present with me. Indra brought Gayatri along and Rudra and Vishnu gave her in marriage to me. Devi, forgive this one act of mine which has caused you so much anger and pain. I will never offend you again.'

But Saraswati could not be appeased so easily. She looked around the assembly, her beautiful eyes blazing with fire, and cursed each and every one of the gods.

First to hear the words of rage was Brahma himself. 'May you never be worshipped in a temple except for one day in a year. Indra, since you brought that milkmaid to Brahma, you shall be bound in chains by your enemies.' Then she turned to Vishnu and said, 'You are the one who gave her in marriage to Brahma so you shall be born amongst men and for long you will wander as the humble keeper of cattle.' To the priests and sages who had witnessed the marriage of Brahma, she said, 'Henceforth you shall perform sacrifices solely from the desire of obtaining gifts, from covetousness shall you attend holy places.' The wives of the gods assembled could not escape her wrath either though they were just innocent bystanders and she raged at them, 'May you all remain barren.' After having pronounced her torrent of curses, Saraswati stormed out of the assembly. Vishnu tried in vain to appease her but the goddess would not listen to him and left. The curses were then modified by Gayatri who gave the assembled gods her blessings.

The Padma Purana gives a different and happier ending to the story.

Brahma did not want Saraswati to leave in such a rage and asked Vishnu and Lakshmi to go with her. 'Ask her to return. Calm her down with soothing words.' After much cajoling, Saraswati's anger finally cooled down and she returned to the assembly of gods. Vishnu had succeeded in appeasing the goddess so well that soon she became her benevolent self and was kind enough to modify her curses. She was then persuaded to give her blessings to all those assembled and Gayatri, who had been standing quietly till now, came and fell at Saraswati's feet. The goddess raised her up and embracing her said, 'A wife ought to obey the wishes and orders of her husband; for that wife who reproaches her husband and who is complaining and quarrelsome shall most assuredly when she dies go to hell. Therefore let us both be attached to Brahma.' Gayatri, happy that the goddess of learning had forgiven her, said, 'So be it. Your orders will I always obey, and esteem your friendship precious as my life. Your daughter am I, O goddess! Deign to protect me.'

Sita

For centuries, Sita, the heroine of the Ramayana, has been the role model for an ideal Hindu wife. One of the most popular heroines in both classical literature and art and in folklore, Sita is revered as a self-sacrificing, loyal wife who is steadfast in her love for her husband despite many hardships.

A tragic heroine of mythology, Sita's life was never easy even in her previous births. Her name Sita means furrow or a line made by the plough and in Vedic literature she was seen originally as a goddess of agriculture. In a hymn from the Rig Veda Sita is invoked with these words:

'Auspicious Sita, come thou near:
We venerate and worship thee
That thou mayst bless and prosper us
and bring us fruits abundantly

'May Indra press the furrow down,
may Pushan guide its course aright.
May she, as rich in milk, be drained for us
through each succeeding year.'

(from *Hindu Goddesses*)

Though her name was invoked during various Vedic rituals and the goddess was associated with thunder and rain, Sita became an important goddess after Valmiki's Ramayana. It is clear in the epic that Sita was not an ordinary mortal and even her birth was ayonija, or not from a womb. Since she is the consort of Rama, an avatar of Vishnu, Sita is considered an avatar of Lakshmi in the Ramayana.

Rama, as it is destined, wins Sita at her swayamvara, a contest for suitors to win the bride, and brings her to Ayodhya as his wife. She follows him to the forest when he is banished, sharing the life of deprivation with him and later when she is abducted by Ravana, she remains chaste and loyal to her husband. Sita's purity, sacrifice and devotion to Rama elevated her position in the galaxy of goddesses, and now she stands on a high pedestal—an ideal

Hindu wife. Though she is never depicted as a powerful goddess like Durga or an independent one like Lakshmi and there are probably no temples dedicated only to her as she is rarely worshipped in her own right, she still remains a popular figure of wifely devotion and loyalty. Every child knows the story of her selfless devotion to Rama, and women are praised for being a 'Sita-like wife'. A verse from the Ramayana, which was spoken for Sita, is sung during wedding ceremonies when the father gives the bride away:

'Here is my daughter, Sita, who will forever walk with you on the path of dharma. Take her hand. Blessed and devoted, she will ever be with you like your own shadow.'

In north India, every autumn, the story of Ramayana is enacted during Ramlila. The role of Sita is played by male actors, and whenever she appears on stage the spectators throw flowers at her feet. Sometimes she is addressed as the mother, who leads her devotees to Rama.

Despite her subordinate position, Sita is depicted as a woman with great strength of character who bore her misfortunes with long-suffering patience and finally decided to depart with dignity from this earthly life.

As an incarnation of Lakshmi, Sita is said to have been born again to take revenge on Ravana who had insulted her in her previous birth. Sita's extraordinary birth is described in this story from the Ramayana.

Ravana, in the course of his wanderings through the world, came to a forest on the Himalayas, where he saw a damsel of brilliant beauty. She was dressed in the robes of an ascetic and lost in deep meditation. Ravana, enamoured by her beauty and simplicity, tells her that she who is so young

and desirable should not be leading a life of austerity. 'Who
are you? Why are you here, in this lonely place?' he asked
her. After some hesitation she replied, 'I am Vedavati, the
daughter of sage Kusadhvaja, sprung from him during his
constant study of the Vedas. The gods wished that I should
choose a husband, but my father would give me to none else
than to Vishnu, the lord of the world, whom he desired for a
son-in-law.' This resolution by Vedavati's father had made
many gods and kings angry. 'Only Lord Vishnu will do
for him. Does the sage, in his arrogance, think us inferior,'
they had muttered. Sambini, the king of the rakshasas, was
so enraged by this that he killed sage Kusadhvaja while he
was asleep. Vedavati's mother, overcome by grief at the loss
of her husband, embraced his body and entered the fire. 'In
order that I may fulfil this desire of my father in respect of
Narayana (Vishnu), I wed him with my heart. After having
done so I practise great austerity. I resort to this severe
observance from the desire of obtaining him,' said Vedavati
returning to her meditation.

But Ravana was not thwarted by her words and pressed
his suit. His passion was not diminished even though
Vedavati refused to look at him. He told her only old
people should practise austerity. 'You who are so young and
beautiful should become my wife. I am Ravana—a great
king and superior to Vishnu,' he boasted. Vedavati replied
that no one can stand before Lord Vishnu and chided him
for speaking thus about her lord. Ravana refused to leave
and moved forward to touch her hair with the tip of his
finger. Vedavati, greatly incensed, cut off her hair at once.
'You vile man. You have insulted me by touching the hair

on my head with your finger. You have shamed me and I can no longer continue to live. I shall enter into the fire at this very moment before your eyes. But hear my word, O arrogant king. Since I have been insulted in the forest by you who are wicked-hearted, I shall be born again for your destruction. For a man of evil design cannot be slain by a woman, and the merit of my austerity will be lost if I were to launch a curse against you. But if I have performed, or bestowed, or sacrificed aught, may I be born a virtuous daughter, not produced by the womb, of a righteous man.' Having thus spoken she entered the blazing fire and a shower of celestial sparks fell from the sky.

The verse then explains the birth of Sita to Rama. 'She it is, lord, who has been born as the daughter of King Janaka and has become thy bride; for thou art the eternal Vishnu. The mountain-like enemy who was virtually destroyed before by her wrath has now been slain by her, having recourse to thy superhuman energy.'

Vedavati was born again as Sita. As predicted, her birth was not from the womb but from the earth itself. King Janaka of Mithila, a noble and virtuous ruler, and a learned king who Krishna cites in the Bhagavad Gita as an illustrious example of a Karma Yogi, was chosen by the gods to be worthy of Sita's father. One day he was ploughing his fields himself to prepare for a sacrifice when he suddenly saw a beautiful girl spring up from the furrow. Janaka accepted the child as goddess earth's gift to him and named the infant girl Sita.

A folk variation of this legend gives an interesting account of how Sita came to be born from the earth.

Vedavati, daughter of sage Kusadhvaja, was born from his mouth while he was chanting the Vedas. She was the incarnation of Lakshmi and soon after she was born her parents regained all the wealth and prosperity they had lost earlier. From a young age she wanted Lord Vishnu to be her husband and prayed to him every day.

An asura named Sambhu came to the hermitage one day and asked her to marry him but when her father did not give his consent, the asura killed him. When Vedavati saw her father lying in a pool of blood, she looked at the asura with anger and rage and he was burnt to ashes at once. Then Vedavati went away to the mountains and began to do severe penance to get Vishnu as her husband.

This was the time when Ravana had begun his campaign of conquests all over the earth. Like a raging fire he stormed through the land, defeating all kings in his way. When he reached the Himalayas, he saw the beautiful Vedavati sitting alone on a mountain peak. He fell in love with her at once and asked her who she was and what she was doing in such a remote place all alone. When Vedavati did not respond to him he boasted, 'I am the mighty ten-headed king of Lanka, Ravana. I have come here after defeating all the kings that stood in my way. I desire to make you my wife. Throw away your garments of bark, let your matted tresses be beautiful again. Adorn yourself in silk and gold. Come with me beautiful maiden. This life is not for you.' His words made no impression on Vedavati who sat quietly chanting her lord's name. Ravana lost his temper and tried to pull her hand. Vedavati immediately bit his hand and fled from the spot.

'You have defiled me and I no longer wish to retain this body touched by your vile hands,' she said and burnt herself right before his eyes. 'I will be born again. Lord Vishnu will be my husband and I will be the cause of your death,' she vowed before she died.

Ravana was astounded by Vedavati's death. 'How lovely she was. I wanted her to be my queen,' he said feeling extremely sad for himself. Then he collected the ashes from the ground with his own hands while his army generals watched in amazement. When he reached Lanka he ordered a golden box to be made in which he put Vedavati's ashes. He chose a quiet place in his palace garden to bury it and used to visit the bower every day to pay his respects to Vedavati. But bad omens began to be seen in Lanka after the arrival of Vedavati's ashes. Floods, famine and death took over the city. One day Narada arrived at the palace and he told Ravana that the cause of these bad omens and ill luck was the golden box of ashes. 'If you keep that box here any longer it will cause great destruction and disaster for your land,' he announced. Ravana's queens, horrified at the thought of the evil shadow the box was casting over their empire, begged him to throw it away. With a heavy heart, Ravana took the golden box of Vedavati's ashes and cast it into the sea. The waves carried the box to the shores of India, where it lay buried in the sand. Then one day, a gang of robbers found the box and carried it away to a forest in the northern part of India. When they were caught by the king's soldiers, one of them hid it under the roots of a tree, hoping to retrieve it later. But the next day the river flooded the forest and the box was carried away to Mithila where it lay under the river basin for some years. This was the very place chosen by King Janaka for a sacrifice. The ashes of Vedavati had mingled with her spirit and formed a female child and this was the child that Janaka found and named Sita.

The story of Sita's wedding to Rama is narrated at great length in the Ramayana and in the Devi Bhagavata Purana. In later periods poets such as Tulasidas wrote beautiful verses describing this episode. Many popular folk tales in various languages celebrate this well-loved story and ballads are sung in villages all over India during the Dussehra festival. 'Sita Swayamvar' attracts a huge crowd when it is enacted during Ramlila and women offer sweets to each other when the wedding takes place on stage.

When Rama was about sixteen years of age, a sage named Vishwamitra came to his father, King Dasharatha, and asked his help to kill two demons named Maricha and Suvahu. Rama and his younger brother Lakshmana set out with the sage to his hermitage in the forest. They soon put an end to the demons and the sage, pleased with them, offered them many boons. The hermits told Rama that they had been invited to a sacrifice which King Janaka of Mithila had organized and asked Rama and Lakshmana to accompany them. They told Rama, who was uncertain about going with them, about the mighty bow which King Janaka possessed. 'A bow which belonged to Shiva himself. It was with this bow that Shiva had created havoc when enraged at the way Sati had been treated by her father Daksha. The bow was a gift from Shiva to Janaka—a reward for a sacrifice. Janaka had declared that he would only give his daughter Sita's hand in marriage to the man who could string this great bow of Shiva's.'

Rama was thus persuaded to accompany the sages to Janaka's court. When the two princes arrived, Janaka was very pleased to see them and offered them the best seat in his court. He showed them the mighty bow and said, 'This heavenly bow, if young Rama's hand can string, to him I shall give, as I have sworn, my daughter Sita, who was not born of a woman.'

The king ordered his men to bring the bow which was kept in an iron box. It was brought to the assembly on an eight-wheeled carriage, a row of men pulling it like a chariot. All the kings and princes gathered at Janaka's court gasped at its immense weight. Those who had some pride decided that they would not even attempt to lift it but some foolish and vain princes strutted up to the box, tightening their belts. One by one they all failed and returned to their seats, their faces burning with shame. Kings, princes, gods and demons in the form of mortal men, they all came and tried their hand but the bow seemed to get heavier. It seemed as if Brahma had not created a single man who could move the bow, leave alone lift and string it.

'I know now that this earth is bereft of brave men. If only I had known this I would have not made this pledge. Now my daughter will remain unmarried because I cannot change my words and lose face,' declared Janaka with sorrow. The entire assembly looked at Sita, seated like a lotus bud amongst them, and felt her father's sadness in their hearts.

When he heard these words, Lakshmana's lips quivered with anger but fearing his older brother he swallowed his words. He laid his head at Rama's feet and said, 'O Rama, how dare anyone utter these words in your presence? Does he not know that you can pick this bow as easily as a lotus stem?' Rama placed his hand on Lakshmana's head with affection and stayed calmly seated. Then Vishwamitra spoke to him. 'Rise, O Rama. Break this mighty bow of Shiva and erase Janaka's plight.' Hearing these words Rama bowed his head to his guru. There was no elation in his heart neither was there any agitation. He stood up and walked towards the bow as graceful as a young lion. Silence fell on the assembly. The sages began to offer prayers in their minds. Sita sat quietly, her heart full of fear and love for Rama. She began to call upon all the gods she could recall at that moment with an agitated mind. 'O Shiva, please shower your blessing on me and take away the weight of this bow. O Ganesha, you give us all boons. Please take away the weight of this bow,' she said over and over again, her eyes filling with tears. 'Why did my father keep such a difficult pledge? This is so unfair. Behold this bow which is like a bolt of lightning and this tender lotus-eyed, dark-skinned boy. How can I sit here patiently and watch what is going to happen? Can a soft siris blossom pierce a diamond? Has everyone lost their senses? O Shiva's mighty bow, now you are my only hope. Cast your heaviness away to the winds and help me,' thought Sita, her eyes restlessly darting about like fish in a pond. Then realizing that her tears would not stop and her heart would not stay calm, Sita spoke these soothing words to herself to quieten her fears: 'If I am true in my spirit, body and words to my lord, then the god who lives in everyone's heart will certainly make me my Lord Rama's slave.' Sita looked at Rama and then cast her eyes down to the ground. 'Those who have true love in their heart will always win the one they love, there is no doubt about that.' She looked at Rama again and decided in her heart to be only his, come whatever may. The moment her shy glance, brimming with love, fell on Rama's face, he knew what was on her mind.

With a quick movement full of grace, he opened the iron box and lifted the bow effortlessly as if it were a garland of flowers. The bow crackled like lightning and its form filled the sky in a blaze of silver. Not one person in the huge assembly saw Rama lift the bow or string it since he moved as swiftly as light, but they heard the roar of thunder that made them tremble with fear. A deafening noise echoed through all the three worlds, the sun's horses left their path and began to run helter-skelter, wild beasts began to howl as the earth swayed. Then everyone cried out 'Hail Rama'. From the sky, music began to play as the apsaras sang and danced.

Sita's happiness knew no bounds as she walked towards Rama, holding the nuptial garland. Though her shyness made her timid, her love for Rama made her heart leap with joy. She knew that her love for him was a secret as yet from her family and none could see it in her heart. But when she reached Rama, Sita was so dazzled by him, that she stood mute, unable to move. Her friends cleverly guessed the turmoil in her heart and whispered, 'O lovely Princess, put the garland around his neck.' Sita, shaken out of her trance, tried to lift her hands but was suddenly so overwhelmed by love that she could not raise her arms. Then as the women began to sing in praise of Rama, Sita managed to put the garland around her beloved Rama with trembling hands. Once more the heavens filled with music as flowers streamed down over the wedded pair. The earth, sky and the underworld rejoiced when they heard that Rama had broken the mighty bow and won Sita's hand. In every home, rich and poor, people lit lamps to show their happiness, while Brahma and a host of other celestial beings showered their blessings on Rama and Sita.

In the Ramayana, as well as in other literature from Hindu mythology, Sita is defined as the ideal wife, whose entire life revolves around her husband. For Sita, Rama is the very essence of life and she always remains faithful to him. Sita's loyalty and devotion to Rama as a pativrata is illustrated by several episodes in the Ramayana.

Rama was exiled to the forest for fourteen years. As he prepared to leave, obeying his father's orders, he told Sita that she could not accompany him as she would not be able to bear the harsh life of the forest. 'You have only known the comfort of a palace and you will not be able to bear the ordeals of a forest life.' Sita, grief-stricken at the thought of life without Rama, said, 'O son of an illustrious monarch, a father, a mother, a brother, a son or a daughter-in-law enjoy the fruit of their merits and receive what is their due, a wife alone follows the destiny of her consort. From now on my duty is clear, I shall dwell in the forest! For a woman, it is not her father, her son, nor her mother, friends nor her own self, but the husband, who in this world and the next is ever her sole means of salvation. If you do enter the impenetrable forest today, O descendant of Raghu, I shall precede you on foot, treading down the spiky kusha grass . . . I shall dwell as willingly in the forest as formerly I inhabited the palace of my father, having no anxiety in the three worlds and reflecting on my duties towards my lord. Ever subject to your will, docile, living like an ascetic in those honey-scented woodlands, I shall be happy in your proximity, O Rama, O Illustrious Lord.'

Rama tried to dissuade her, telling her that it was not safe for her to be in the forest where there were wild beasts and demons and he could not bear to inflict such a hardship on her. 'I have to obey my father's wishes, but why should you give up your comfortable life here. You will be safer and happier living in the palace with your father-in-law and mother-in-law instead of living a harsh life in the forest with me,' he said. But Sita though docile and timid showed a firm resolve which astounded everyone. 'The hardships described by you will be transmuted into joys through my devotion to you. If I am ever separated from you I shall immediately yield up my life. Without her consort, a woman cannot live, you cannot doubt this truth where I am concerned. O pure-souled one, I shall remain sinless by following piously in the steps of my consort, for a husband is a god.'

Thus Sita convinced Rama to allow her to go with him. They lived in the forest happily for a while, enjoying the simple life in their hut in Chitrakoot. Then one day Ravana's shadow fell once more on Sita. She was abducted by him and taken to Lanka.

This episode from the *Ramcharitmanas* describes Sita's grief at being parted from Rama.

Abducted by Ravana and taken to Lanka, Sita was kept as a prisoner in a garden full of ashoka trees.

Sita sat under the shade of an ashoka tree with her eyes downcast and her heart filled with sorrow. She did not look up when Ravana, accompanied by his wives, came and stood before her. 'Raise your eyes, lovely woman. Look up at me just once and I will give you all the wealth in the world. My love for you is limitless. I have everything in the world, wealth, fame, power yet I humble myself before you. I am the king of demons and I could take you by force, but I do not want to do that. Agree to be mine, I will make these queens of mine your slaves. Marry me and you will be the queen of the world,' he said, but Sita did not lift her face. 'Marry me, you proud and obstinate woman, or else I will kill you,' he roared. Sita then spoke in a quiet voice, keeping her face hidden from Ravana. 'Can a lotus flower in the light of a lowly glowworm? You evil man, have you no fear of Lord Rama's lethal arrow? You have brought me here by deceit. You are not a mighty king but a coward who steals helpless women when their menfolk are away. Are you not ashamed of yourself? Even a snake is better than you that crawls on the ground.' Ravana was stunned by Sita's insulting words. None had ever dared to speak to him like this and abuse him in the presence of his queens. He drew his sword in fury and rushed towards Sita. 'I will kill you here and now, you have insulted me. Listen woman, marry me at once, or I will cut your head off and slice your body into pieces with this sword of mine which has seen only victory in battle.'

'Kill me then,' said Sita, 'I will prefer to die by this cold and clean sword to suffering this terrible fire of agony which has been burning in me ever since I have been separated from my lord.' As Ravana was about to raise his sword, his wife Mandodari stopped him. 'It is wrong for you—a great warrior—to slay a woman. It is against all norms. Restrain your anger, mighty King of Lanka. Remember your glory in this kingdom of yours,' she said.

Though Ravana was fuming with rage he had to listen to his wife's wise words. He looked down at Sita angrily and said, 'I give you a month to make up your mind to marry me. If you do not agree, you will be put to death,' and stormed out of the ashoka garden. As soon as he left, all the demonesses who had been left to guard Sita began harassing her, whispering cruel words into her ears. They took on horrible forms and attacked her from all sides, trying to frighten her into accepting Ravana's proposal. Sita covered her face in her arms and meditated upon an image of Rama. Her doe eyes which had been filled with tears gradually cleared as she thought of her beloved Rama and her heart, though heavy with sorrow, felt joyous as her mind shone with her lord's form.

Just then one of the demonesses, Trijata, who secretly worshipped Rama, came forward and spoke to the others. 'Gather around me and listen. I had a dream last night which you should pay attention to because it will soon come true. I dreamt last night that a giant of a monkey has burnt our Lanka and killed our entire army of mighty demons. Ravana, our king, is naked and all his heads are shaven. I saw him heading towards the land of the dead, riding a donkey, his twenty arms cut off. As he leaves, I saw Vibhishan being crowned our king and the entire land singing Rama's name. Then the lord calls Sita to him. Believe in this dream of mine because I swear it will come true within a few days.'

When the demonesses heard Trijata's words, they were frightened and fell at Sita's feet, asking for her forgiveness. Then they all ran away, leaving Sita alone in the ashoka garden with only Trijata. Sita, afraid that a month would soon be over, asked Trijata to help her. 'You are my friend in this hour of my ordeal. Help me, kind friend, to put an end to this endless life of sorrow. Bring some firewood and make a funeral pyre and light it for me. I cannot bear to hear Ravana's voice again.' Trijata touched Sita's feet and soothed her with kind words. She reminded her of Rama's glory, strength and valour and then, as night fell, she went away leaving Sita alone.

'What shall I do to end this burden of grief? Where shall I get the fire to erase this sorrow?' cried Sita looking up at the night sky. 'The sky is filled with flames but not one star falls on earth. The moon too is full of fire but it does not shower its burning arrows on an unfortunate woman like me. Listen to me, O ashoka trees. Take my sorrow away so that you become true to your names. Your tender green leaves are like embers of fire. Shower them on me and reach this grief to its end.'

Hanuman, who had been hiding in the trees till then, threw her a ring which belonged to Rama. Sita, thinking the ashoka tree had thrown her a bit of flame, put her hand out quickly and picked it up. When she saw it was Rama's ring, her heart leapt with joy at first and then was filled with fear. 'How can his ring be here? No, nothing can happen to my lord. He is invincible in this world, who can defeat him? But who can make a ring like this which only belongs to him?' Anxious thoughts raced through Sita's mind. Then Hanuman, who knew now that he had to convince Sita of Rama's well-being, began singing Rama's praises. He sang sweetly of all the noble deeds Rama had done from the time he was a young boy. He sang about Rama's great beauty, his valour, and as soon as Sita heard the words describing her husband's glory, her heart was at peace. 'Come forward whoever you are. Why do you not show yourself?' she asked, looking up at the ashoka trees. Hanuman jumped down to reveal himself, much to Sita's surprise. What was this? A monkey who sang her lord's praises? Where has he come from, she thought. Hanuman, by then certain that this was Sita and no other, came and bowed before her. 'O Mother Sita, I am your Lord Rama's messenger. He gave me this ring to give to you,' he said and explained how he had come to meet Rama. Once Sita knew that Hanuman was truly Rama's messenger, she began asking him about her lord.

'O Hanuman, I was drowning in this sea of grief but you have appeared like a ship to save me. Tell me, does my lord think of me? Will my eyes ever find solace in that dark, gentle image?' Sita was choking with sorrow and her eyes filled with tears. 'O my lord, have you totally forsaken me?' she cried. Hanuman could not bear to see Sita's grief and spoke to her in a gentle voice. 'He is well in body but his heart is full of sorrow. Do not make yourself unhappy. Rama's love for you is as great as yours for him. Have patience and listen to his message which I will now relate to you, mother,' and folding his hands in prayer Hanuman began to recite Rama's message to Sita. 'These are his words spoken for you, "O Sita, in your absence everything has turned contrary for me. The new leaves of a tree are like flames, the gentle moon like the fierce sun, a lotus blossom as sharp as a spear. It seems to me as if the clouds are pouring boiling oil on earth and those who cared for me once now only make me suffer. The fragrant, cool winds that once blew in this land have now become hot and poisonous. They say that if you speak of your grief to someone it may become easier to bear it, but who will I speak to. There is none who knows the intensity and depth of our love except my mind, and my mind is forever with you, my love. With this, understand in your heart the love I have for you."'

When Sita heard these words, she was so overwhelmed with love for Rama that she forgot everything and lost herself totally, thinking of her beloved Rama. Then she opened her tear-filled doe eyes and spoke to Hanuman, 'You bring me a message which gives both bliss and pain. Bliss, because I still abide in his heart; pain, as he wakes and weeps far from me.'

When Sita was finally rescued by Rama and Lakshmana and their vast army of valiant monkeys, instead of a joyous meeting with Rama, she was greeted coldly by her husband. In this episode from the Ramayana, Sita is made to go through an ordeal by fire to prove her innocence.

After the battle was over, Sita waited. This was the moment she had longed for. But why was it not as joyous as she had envisioned it would be? Rama, who she thought she would never see again, for whom her heart cried every night, stood before her like a stranger. It was as if he had never seen her before and had nothing to do with her. He gazed upon her and spoke in an unfamiliar, cold voice. 'I have won you, fair lady, by conquering my enemy in battle,' said Rama. 'I have obliterated the dishonour that was upon me and vanquished my enemy with the help of these brave monkeys. Today the black shadow cast upon my family honour has been erased. I have done all that a man should do to wipe out an intolerable insult at the hands of an enemy. I won you, Sita, as every man should fight to protect his wife. But let it be known that this great battle accomplished by means of heroism of my friends was not undertaken by me for your sake. It was not love for you that led my army over the sea. I battled to avenge the cause of honour and insult.'

Sita looked at him, bewildered by his harsh words. Could this really be true, she thought, gazing upon her husband. 'Is this really his voice that attacks me thus like a shower of arrows? Why does he speak these harsh words to me before this vast army of monkeys and demons?' Then Rama continued, keeping his face averted from her face. 'But as you stand before me, doubts have arisen about your behaviour. What man of good family can take back his wife after she has lived in another man's house for so long? Should he compromise his honour, his family's good name just because he longs for her? Sita, go away from me. Go and live wherever you wish but do not stand before me. I no longer wish to see you.'

Sita, deeply ashamed and trembling with sorrow, tried to speak to him. Her beautiful face was wet with tears and Rama's voice, harsh and unfamiliar, echoed in her ears, filling her with a deep sadness.

Then he spoke to her again. 'Go. Go at once. Choose any place and I will see you are reached there. Just understand that you cannot live with me. You may be my wife but you have lived under Ravana's care for so long. He must have gazed upon your beautiful face so many times, tried to put his arms around your waist. You are tainted by his evil touch. I cannot accept you as my wife any more. Leave me since I do not wish to see you ever again.'

Sita stood still as her husband accused her with these cruel words in front of the entire army. Her eyes full of tears, she tried once again to speak to Rama, to tell him that she was innocent. 'Why do you accuse me in this heartless way? I have done no wrong. I am as chaste and pure as I always was. Believe me, my lord, I have not behaved in any improper way. My heart is ever attached to you. My eyes see nothing but your face. My ears hear no voice but yours. Do not cast me aside like this. I cannot live without you,' she cried, but Rama turned his face away. 'If you wanted to discard me why did you send Hanuman with your ring? Why did you give me hope to live on? I was quite willing to die when my heart was breaking with sorrow, when I thought I would never set eyes upon you again. I know now that death is the only way out for me. Discarded by you, tainted by false accusations, I do not wish to live. Build a pyre for me. By entering the fire I will end this life of sorrow. Fire shall be my solace,' said Sita.

Lakshmana and Hanuman, who were standing nearby, tried to persuade Rama to take Sita back. 'She is as pure as the earth and the sky,' they said, but Rama showed no signs of forgiving her. He ordered Lakshmana to build a pyre for Sita. As the monkeys and demons watched, Sita folded her hands and prayed to the fire. 'As my heart never wavered for even a moment from the image of Rama, fire that purifies all, protect my honour.' And then she walked around the pyre and stepped into the blazing fire.

As soon as the flames touched her body, all the people who were watching, the army of monkeys and rakshasas began to wail loudly. Lakshmana, Hanuman and many of the vanquished demons too cried out in horror. They begged Rama to save Sita from this cruel fate. But Rama did not even look towards the burning pyre.

But as the fire burned, sending its flames high into the sky, they saw an amazing sight. Sita sat in the middle of the raging fire but somehow her beautiful form remained intact. The flames rose around her in a golden circle but they did not touch her. Her lovely face, her graceful body, her hair shone as before and her clothes too retained their lustre. One by one the gods began to descend from heaven. Kubera, Yama, Indra, Varuna, Shiva and Brahma and many other gods came down in their celestial chariots that shone like the sun. They approached Rama who stood before them with his palms joined, eyes cast down respectfully, and said, 'How can you give Sita, who is so pure and chaste, to the fire? Do you not recognize her true nature?'

Rama replied in a soft voice that he considered himself only a mortal. Hearing this, Brahma explained to him that he was the incarnation of Vishnu, born on earth to slay Ravana, and Sita, his wife, was the incarnation of goddess Lakshmi. When Agni, the god of fire, heard Brahma's words, he rose up, holding Sita like a precious gem. Sita now shone like the morning sun, her hair dark and flowing, adorned with golden ornaments that had been purified by the fire. Agni placed her in Rama's lap and said to him in a forceful voice that echoed in all the three worlds, 'Here is your Sita, your beloved wife. There is no evil in her, neither in speech nor in mind, nor in thought, nor in glance. She is the most virtuous of all wives. She has never thought of anything else but you and prayed for your safety. She has suffered due to no fault of hers and even then her thoughts were never against anyone. When you left her alone in the deserted forest, and she was miserable and powerless, she was carried away by the rakshasa Ravana, who wanted to avenge an insult to his sister. She remained forever loyal to you. Though Sita was imprisoned and hidden away in a dark corner, her thoughts were always on you. She was guarded day and night by deformed, hideous rakshasa women. She was tempted and threatened, yet she never even looked at that evil Ravana, for she belonged with her entire being only to you. Accept her, for she is pure and chaste.' Agni declared this, his flames dancing around Sita and Rama.

Rama heard him in silence and then he spoke to all the assembled gods. 'It was necessary that Sita should enter the purifying fire in the presence of all the people of the world. She had lived long in the house of Ravana and if I had taken her back at once what would the people think of me? Would they not say that Rama, the son of Dasharatha, is lustful and childish? I know well that Sita, daughter of noble King Janaka, has given her heart to no other, that she is devoted and has kept her thoughts always upon me, but in order to convince the people that she spoke the truth, I had to spurn her publicly.' Then, as the demons and the monkeys rejoiced, he took Sita's hand and led her to his chariot.

But Sita was not destined to live happily ever after. In Uttara Khand of the Ramayana, which many believe was not Valmiki's creation, Sita is once again made to enter the fire to prove her innocence but this time she does not return to life. Unable to bear her endless sorrow, she asks the earth which gave her birth to open and receive her once more. And then Sita, the most chaste and pious wife, disappears forever into the lap of her mother.

Radha

Radha's name is inseparable from Krishna's in Hindu mythology, yet she is not found anywhere in the most important Purana dedicated to Lord Krishna—the Bhagavata Purana. There are a few lines about a gopi who was chosen amongst all the other gopis to accompany Krishna into the forest.

'Her heart swollen with vanity since now she considered herself the best of womankind, the gopi asked Sri Krishna to carry her. He agreed and asked her to climb onto his shoulders but as soon as she touched him he vanished into the air leaving her humiliated and repentant.' Later works consider this gopi to be Radha and gradually over the years many wonderful tales of love were woven around her and her beloved Krishna.

There are various versions given about the origin of Radha in the later Puranas. According to the Padma Purana, she appeared as a bhumi-kanya, earth-girl, when King Vrishabhanu was preparing the ground for a yagna, but the Brahmavaivarta Purana, giving a lengthy account of Radha's birth, says that she was born in Gokula as the daughter of Kalavati and Vrishabhanu. The text also says that she was born from the left side of Krishna. In the Devi Bhagavata Purana, Radha is considered one of the five forces which helped Lord Vishnu in the process of creation. Narayana makes an obeisance to Radha with these words in the Devi Bhagavata Purana:

'Salutation to thee the supreme goddess, who resides at rasamandala, who lords over rasa and is dearer to Krishna than his own life. Salutations to the mother of all the three worlds, whose lotus-like feet are worshipped by gods headed by Brahma and Vishnu. Be propitiated, O Ocean of Mercy.'

Radha, like Sita, is seen primarily in relation to a male consort though there are religious sects in Bengal and Uttar Pradesh which worship her as an independent goddess. Unlike Sita, Radha's relationship with Krishna is not as a devoted wife. Instead, she gives herself up totally to form an illicit relationship with her beloved. Radha's love for Krishna is an obsession which makes her break all norms of society and disregard her family to be with her divine lover. Radha and Krishna's love tales take place during Krishna's youth in the village of cowherds in Vraja and in the romantic woods of Vrindavan. Radha's love life is full of highs and lows as she hovers between despair and ecstasy. Krishna loves her with true passion, yet he cannot help sporting with the other gopis just to torment her. She is his favourite, but their love play is full of jealousy and longing.

In the *Gitagovinda*, a beautiful poem composed by Jayadeva during the twelfth century, we see Radha as a fully developed personality for the first time. The theme of the poem is Radha's intense love and longing for Krishna, her total devotion to him, regardless of anything else. This powerful love relationship of Radha and Krishna is seen as a metaphor for the divine-human relationship, with Radha representing the human devotee who gives up her entire being to be one with god.

In the *Gitagovinda*, Radha is seen as a lovelorn heroine, always pining for her lover. The dominant emotion of this great poetic work is viraha ras, or love in separation. In lyrical verse, the poet describes Radha's longing for Krishna, her jealousy and sorrow. She loves him with all her heart, defying society, against her own will even though he is not always faithful to her.

'My mind counts the multitude of his virtues, it does not think of his roaming even by mistake, and it possesses delight, it pardons him his transgressions from afar; even when fickle Krishna delights among the girls without me, yet again my perverse mind loves him! What am I to do?'

Radha is a married woman and in some Puranic texts older than Krishna. Her illicit love for Krishna and its power as a religious metaphor fascinated many poets in the thirteenth and fourteenth centuries. In their works, we see Radha as a tragic heroine torn between her overwhelming love for Krishna and her reputation as a respectable wife. She knows how dangerous it is for her to indulge in this secret loveplay. She has no formal claim on her beloved and can only meet him secretly in the darkness, hiding in the woods of Vrindavan. For every tryst with her lover she must risk the dangers of the night, the lonely woods and the disapproval of the village society.

'If I go to Krishna I lose my home
If I stay I lose my love'

Radha's tormented love for Krishna inspired the fourteenth-century poet Chandidas to say:

'I who body and soul
am at your beck and call,
was a girl of noble family.
I took no thought for what would be said of me,
I abandoned everything.'

Radha's love for Krishna is praised by poets as the purest form of divine love. To this day, Krishna devotees consider Radha's love for Krishna as selfless love which expresses itself without any formal obligations on her part. She goes against the ways of the world to express her love and hopes to gain nothing. Radha loves Krishna in spite of everything just as a true devotee should.

Radha is considered by the poets as the ideal of feminine beauty which was described in the epics. She follows the same image as Sita and Draupadi and like them she too is slender, with limbs as delicate as spring blossoms. Her eyes, hands and feet are like lotuses and her breasts round and swelling, her thighs firm and hard, her lower lip like the sweet red bimba fruit, her hair dark and curly, her brows curved like serpents. The poet Jayadeva, who was an ardent Krishna devotee and faced many hardships because of his single-minded devotion, gives a beautiful and poignant description of Krishna's love for Radha.

'The pleasures of her touch and the tremulous, tender wandering of her eyes, the fragrance of the lotus which is her mouth, the cunning flow of the nectar of her words, the mead from her bimba-like lower lip—if thus, even in attachment to sense objects, my mind is fixed in the highest meditation upon her, alas, how then can the sickness of love-in-separation increase.'

In the *Gitagovinda*, Radha is depicted as a passionate, proud woman who is often distraught despite being loved by Krishna since she cannot accept the fact that he belongs to the other gopis as well. Her anger makes her torment herself even when her beloved is with her. 'When the beloved Krishna is tender you Radha are rough, when he bends down in obeisance you are unbending, when he is passionate, you are hostile, when he has his face raised in expectation you have your face turned away . . . O perverse woman . . .'

The endless see-saw of Radha's love life, her emotional traumas of a love-sick heart, was seen as a metaphor for an unhappy devotee who could not find the lord even though she searches relentlessly to unite with him. In later texts, however, Radha's position is elevated and she is seen as Krishna's only beloved, his chosen lover. Exultant and flushed with joy she tells him in a poem by Surdas, 'You become Radha and I will become Madhava.' In another verse Krishna says to her,

'As you are, so am I; there is certainly no difference between us.

As whiteness inheres in milk, as burning in fire, my fair lady,

As smell in earth, so do I inhere in you always.'

In this story from the Brahmavaivarta Purana which considers Radha a goddess, we see her as Krishna's partner. But her life of trauma begins due to a curse.

Radha and Krishna lived and loved in a celestial city of incredible beauty called Goloka—the Cow-world—which was higher than Vaikunth, Vishnu's abode. This lovely place which was devoid of mental or bodily pain, disease, death, sorrow or fear was where silvery rivers flowed and woods were full of cooing doves and dancing peacocks. Here Radha danced like a queen with her beloved Krishna. She knew in her heart that she was the chosen one and belonged body and soul to the lord. The great Brahma himself had proclaimed to Radha, 'You are the outcome of the body of Krishna and equal to him in every respect. No one can say which of you is Radha or Krishna. He represents the soul of the world and you are its body and receptacle.' Time flowed endlessly here with no days and nights separating them as Sri Krishna, bedecked in a yellow dress as bright and pure as fire and ornaments of gold, his brow decorated with sandal paste, his neck adorned with wreaths of pearls, sported with Radha in an endlessly ecstatic dance. Radha, shining like a diamond necklace on Krishna's body, was the mistress of Rasa, and served her lord.

Everything was perfect in this never-ending blissful state as Radha and Krishna sported in Goloka. They danced their eternal dance watched by the other gods. Sometimes the pair hid in the emerald bowers like two doves and then again they emerged to dazzle everyone with their lustre. Hundreds of years went by thus and then one day the dark clouds began to gather. Radha held her breath and watched the darkening sky. She knew in her heart that her life of endless joy was about to be broken by someone. The days of bliss were now over and she could feel a new sense overwhelming her body. 'Is this called fear?' she asked herself.

Then came the day of sorrow which she had been expecting. Sudama, a childhood friend of Krishna, angered by her sudden jealousy over another gopi, cursed her after a bitter quarrel. 'You will descend to the earth and be born a woman,' he said, anger blazing in his eyes. 'You will wander the earth as a common milkmaid. Thus you shall fall from your exalted position as a result of your jealous heart and this curse of mine.'

Radha heard these words and turned to Krishna, 'O destroyer of fear. How shall I bear this curse? How can I live without you even for a moment? You are my life, soul, vision and I am merely the body. My master, I cannot live without serving you. I shall surely die.' Lord Krishna, who knew what was to happen, consoled her. 'Fair one, in the Varaha age I shall descend to the earth. It has been predestined that you will go with me and be born on earth. Goddess, there I shall go and make merry with you in the forest of Vraja. Why should you fear, my beloved, when I am by your side?'

Thus Radha came to be born in Gokula as the daughter of Vrishabhanu. At the age of twelve she was married to Ayana, the brother of Krishna's foster mother, Yashoda.

An episode from the Brahmavaivarta Purana tells us that the marriage of Radha to Ayana was just a game of illusion. Radha's shadow was wedded to Ayana and she was actually Krishna's bride. The following legend describes their first encounter.

Krishna was born, as ordained, in the house of Nanda and Yashoda a few years after Radha had been born in Gokula. One day Nanda had taken his baby son to the forest to graze the cows. Suddenly, through the illusion and supernatural powers of baby Krishna, the sky became overcast and the forest assumed a fearful dark-blue light. Thunder crashed around them furiously and streaks of lightning struck the trees in the forest, making them sway dangerously. Nanda, distraught, ran about collecting his scattered herd and did not know how to manage the baby Krishna. Just then, by good fortune or by Krishna's desire, Radha happened to come by. 'Fear not. I will take care of your son,' she said. A swift dart of light fell on her from the sky as she took the child from Nanda and carried him to a bower of flowers. Radha's beautiful face began to glow as if her features were touched by a golden light. A fragrance of musk rose from her body and her mind was filled with a strange longing. As Radha clasped the baby Krishna to her breast she was reminded of her former life. With a thrill of rapture she remembered the sphere of rasa, the bed made of flowers inside a mansion built with gems. Then as she shut her eyes and recalled her past life, she was surprised to hear the sound of Krishna's laughter. She remembered that he had once been her divine lover. Aching with love, she opened her eyes and found a young boy by her side. His skin was dark blue, his eyes as beautiful as buds. His face seemed to have stolen the beauty of the full moon. Radha gazed at him in wonder.

They looked at each other in love and then Lord Krishna, smiling, said to Radha, 'My beloved, recollect the days of Goloka. I must fulfil the promise I made to you. You are dearer to me than my life. You are the container of the world and I am the cause. Therefore, O chaste one, come and occupy my heart. As an ornament bedecks the body, come and adorn me.'

Then Krishna lifted Radha's face to his and looked at her with love. 'Remember how we played under the flower-filled bowers; how we chased the moonbeams from our heads? I must fulfil the promise I made to you. You are dearer to me than my life. Let us dance the dance of eternal love once more.' As his honeyed voice filled Radha with ecstasy, suddenly Lord Brahma, the priest of the gods, appeared, wishing to perform a marriage ceremony for them. The sound of trumpets and drums came from the skies along with a shower of flowers as he married them and went back to heaven.

When Radha and Krishna were alone, she gently applied a paste of aloe and sandalwood, saffron and musk on his chest and Lord Krishna held Radha by the hand, embraced and kissed her and loosened the cloth which covered her body. All the cosmetics she had applied to make herself even more beautiful were wiped out by Krishna's embrace. The red hue of her lips was removed by his kisses, the chignon was unravelled, the lac-dye on her feet and the vermilion on her hair were smeared as Krishna made love to her. A small bell worn by Radha around her waist as an ornament was torn from her body by the passionate embraces of her lover. Radha lost her reason and could not distinguish day from night as thrills of rapture flooded her body. But then, later on, as she recovered her senses and looked up shyly at Krishna, he was no longer there. In an instant he had taken the form of the infant again and was now crying with hunger. He was exactly in the same place as Nanda had left him and Radha picked him gently in her arms. Tears flowed down her cheeks as she ran as swiftly as she could to Nanda's house. Yashoda was waiting outside the door looking up at the darkening sky with a worried face. She was overjoyed to see Radha with baby Krishna in her arms. 'Take him, he is hungry for milk. I must go home now, I have been away for so long,' said Radha and turned towards her home. But her heart was not sad any more because she knew that from now on she would see her beloved every day. Every day she would go to the sphere of rasa to dance the rasalila with Krishna. Had he not promised to her in another life: 'In the sphere of the rasa, you will sport with me . . . As I am, so you are . . . I constitute your life and you constitute my life . . .'

And so their eternal play continued and they lost themselves in the rapture of their dance, producing a flow of bliss for all the people of the earth who heard the call of Krishna's flute as it sang for Radha.

Radha's love for Krishna was a secret between them and she had to steal out at night to meet him. The poets were very taken by this adulterous, secret love and idealized it. Radha was called a parakiya, or another man's woman. If there is no parakiya there can be no birth of bhava. It is in fear of separation that grief and passionate longing grow.

Every night Radha goes out in secrecy and darkness wearing a dark cloak and silencing her ornaments. 'Abandon the noisy, capricious anklet, go to the dense dark grove; wear a dark blue cloak,' wrote Jayadeva. Radha is not afraid of the dark night, what she fears is not finding Krishna. 'I went to his hut in the secret thicket; secretly at night he remained hiding; I looked fearfully in all directions; he laughed with an abundance of passion for the pleasure-of-love.'

Every night Radha would wait for her husband and mother-in-law to fall asleep and then creep out silently through the door like a thief. She was not afraid of the dark because it helped to hide her but she feared the villagers who might be awake at this late hour. She was also afraid of the evil spirits that lurked in the forest but she thought of Krishna waiting for her and ran towards the dark woods. She could hear his flute now playing faintly from behind a mango grove and the sweet sound made her faint with love. Then suddenly Krishna caught her in his arms, merging his blue skin with her milky white softness. They spent a magical night together, dancing the eternal dance of love as the gods watched from heaven. Then Radha, tired by his passionate lovemaking would lie in his arms, lulled to sleep by the sound of his flute.

Radha's absence from the house at night was noticed by her mother-in-law, Jatila, who had been watching her for some time. The dark shadows under her eyes, her languorous yawns made her suspect Radha had a secret lover. 'My son is never with her either at night or during the day yet she glows with love,' thought Jatila and decided to follow her one night. The moon rose early that night, reaching high above the forest from where it cast its silvery light over the paths. The trees gleamed like white arrows which had been struck by some warrior on the ground. 'O! Why do you shine tonight with such fervour? Have you too turned against my love? See how your light makes the path to the forest so clear and my way so dangerous. Can you not hide your bright face for a few moments behind a dark cloud so that I can run swiftly to my love?' said Radha. Then suddenly she heard footsteps behind her. She tried to run faster but a thorny bush caught her cloak and just then her mother-in-law appeared from behind a tree. 'O Radha, tell us where you are going at this late hour when the whole world is asleep. Tell us, girl, who awaits you in that dark forest where even brave men are afraid of venturing in full daylight? Speak the truth. We wait to hear your voice, your husband, these good women from our village and I,' cried Jatila angrily. Radha, wrenching her cloak free, began to run towards the forest. 'Wait, tell us where you are going,' shouted her husband trying to catch her hand. 'I am going to pray to the goddess Katyayani,' said Radha. 'I do that every night. She stands beneath a bower beyond that hill. I take her fruits and flowers each night,' Radha's heart beat with fear.

'But you carry no fruits or flowers girl,' said a woman, peering at her through the trees. 'I will gather them now. I must go or the auspicious hour will pass,' said Radha as she ran ahead. Krishna was waiting for her near the bower, his blue form glowing like a precious gem. A fragrance of sweet champa blossoms floated in the air. Radha fell into his arms crying with fear. 'O my love, I have told such lies. I told them I was going to pray to Katyayani. What shall I do now?'

Krishna caressed Radha's hair, soothing her trembling body with his gentle touch. 'Then you shall pray to Katyayani, my beloved,' he said and laughed. With a flash of brilliant light which blazed right up to the sky, frightening all the creatures in the forest, shaking the earth violently, Krishna transformed himself into the goddess Katyayani.

When Jatila, Ayana and the village women reached the bower beneath the hill, they saw Radha bowing before the goddess. Flowers of different colours and fresh fruits lay by her as she prayed with her eyes shut. A strange blue light surrounded Radha as if the goddess was blessing her. Ashamed that they had suspected her, everyone went away, leaving Radha alone with her divine lover.

Radha, unlike most goddesses, does not possess a gentle, placid nature. Her proud and passionate image is celebrated in popular legends, poetry as well as in miniature painting and dance. This legend speaks about her intense jealousy and pride which constantly torments her relationship with Krishna. This too is seen by Krishna's devotees as a token of extreme love and passion for the playful, cowherd god.

The day had passed full of sorrow and evening brought no respite. Radha searched every part of Vrindavan, every shade-giving tree, every bower full of flowers but she could not find Krishna anywhere. 'Where has he gone? Find him for me, dear friend, or I shall die of a broken heart,' she lamented to one of the gopis. Her hair, unadorned with flowers or jewels, streamed down like a turbulent river down her back, tears smeared the kohl in her eyes as she ran about like a mad woman, looking for Krishna. Finally a gopi took pity on her and told her the cruel truth. 'He has gone away with Chandravali—the gopi who has caught his eye with her flirtatious, bold manner. It is not his fault,' said the gopi, holding a trembling Radha in her arms. Radha's pain which pierced her heart like a poison-tipped arrow made her want to cry out but she was silent. She quietly returned to her house, keeping her face, racked with sorrow, hidden from passers-by.

All through the night she wept silently, thinking about her beloved Krishna and Chandravali. She imagined him caressing Chandravali just the way he caressed and kissed her and her heart filled with anger. 'He touches her lips with the same soft touch as he did mine. O cruel love, do you remember me at all as you make love to her? Or has she erased all memory of our love from your heart?' she cried as the image of Krishna hovered above her, making her even more distraught. 'Will this night of sorrow never end? Will the moon never leave the sky? Do you linger on tonight, prolonging the hours of darkness because my love is making love to her?' she said, watching the moon through tearful eyes. Finally dawn touched the groves of Vrindavan and Radha went out to milk the cows. There, standing like a glowing flame of blue and gold, was Krishna. He smiled his heartbreaking smile, but Radha's anger now blazed out of her eyes as she beheld her beloved's face. His cheeks, which she loved to kiss, were besmeared with mascara from the other one's eyes. Vermilion streaks marked his chest and his lower lip was red and swollen with teeth-marks—a sign of the other one's passion. Radha's heart filled with anger and pain as she turned away, but Krishna's eyes, red from a sleepless night, would not leave her face. 'How he humiliates me by standing there, so openly showing the marks of his lovemaking on his body. Although he is guilty, he is not afraid; although he is threatened, he is not ashamed; although his crime is visible, he lies about it,' writes Jayadeva, describing Radha's anguish.

Radha finally controls her rage which was making her tremble and finds the strength to speak. 'You made me promises which you forgot when you saw her. You were to be with me and yet you spent the night with her. You are a pitiless, false lover. You make me burn with sorrow,' she said. Krishna tried to placate her with loving words and caresses but she would not stay and listen. Seething with anger and humiliation, she turned away from him and walked home.

Next day a sadhu came to beg at Radha's house. Her mother-in-law and some younger girls went to give him alms but he refused. 'I will only take food from the hands of a woman whose husband is alive. Otherwise I will go away empty-handed from this house,' he said in a loud voice.

Radha's mother-in-law, worried, quickly sent for Radha. 'Come, quickly. Bring some fruits and grain for this holy man. He should not go away from our house empty-handed.' Radha, weak and ill with an aching heart, refused to come out. Other members of the family grew agitated at her refusal and begged her again and again to come out. Radha finally stepped out reluctantly with some food but the holy man refused to take it. 'You must give me what I want,' he said. Radha, surprised, looked up at the holy man. She saw Krishna standing before her, resplendent in a saffron robe. None else could recognize him and her mother-in-law said to Radha, 'Yes, Radha, give him what he asks for. Then he will bless this house. Do not refuse him.' Radha, bewildered, did not know what to do. She could not refuse him since he was dressed like a holy man. 'What do you want from me?' she asked in a low voice. Krishna raised his eyes and looked at her with love. 'I want your pride.' Radha burst into tears as her love for Krishna overwhelmed her once more. Her aching heart was healed with the soothing touch of his loving glance as he took the offered fruits and left, promising to meet her in the bower at night.

Ganga

Ganga, rising from the snowy Himalayas and flowing down many miles into the Bay of Bengal, is considered to be one of the most important rivers of India. A subject of many myths, hymns, folk tales, popular songs and old sculpture panels, she is accorded the status of a goddess and is mentioned in many Puranas and in the Ramayana and the Mahabharata. Her divine origin endows her waters with the powers of cleansing all sins from the past, present and the future. During various auspicious days, thousands of people bathe in her waters in the holy cities like Haridwar, Rishikesh, Prayag and Varanasi. On her banks, the Kumbh Mela, considered to be the largest gathering of people in the world, is held where pilgrims offer prayers to the river. Most devout Hindus make the journey to the Ganga to scatter the ashes of relatives who have died, in the hope that the Ganga will absolve their spirits and make their journey to heaven easier.

The Mahabharata describes the virtues of Ganga with these words: 'If after death, the bones of the dead are deposited in Ganga the departed will attain heaven. Even if one has sinned throughout his life he would attain Vishnupada (heaven) if he worshipped Ganga. Bathing in the Ganga is as beneficial as performing a hundred yagnas. As long as the bones of one remains in the waters of the Ganga so long will he occupy an honourable seat in heaven. He who has come in contact with its water will shine forth as the sun, devoid of all darkness. Places which are not favoured by its waters will become barren like night without the moon and trees without flowers. Ganga water is more than enough to satisfy living things in all the three worlds.'

The Agni Purana too describes the greatness of the river: 'Through whatever places the Ganga flows those places become sublime and sacred. Ganga is the refuge of all created beings who aspire for the final good.' The heavenly Ganga is depicted in art as white in colour, and holding a lotus flower and a pot in her hands, she rests on a fish-like creature called the makaramatsya. Her image is often placed on temple doorways along with Yamuna.

In this tale from the Ramayana Ganga descends from heaven somewhat reluctantly.

There was once a mighty king of Ayodhya named Sagara who was childless. Anxious of having a son who would carry on his line, the king decided to do severe penance for a thousand years. At last, pleased with his worship, the saint Bhrigu granted him his wish. 'One of your queens will have one son who will carry on your name and the other shall have sixty thousand sons.' Soon the elder queen gave birth to a handsome son who was named Anshuman, while the younger queen produced a gourd. Just when she was praying to the gods in despair at not having had a single child, leave alone sixty thousand, the gourd burst into two parts. Out of its rind came sixty thousand babies who were carefully placed in jars of oil. They stayed in their dark retreats till they became young men. Then they rose up, all sixty thousand brothers, and stormed into the light like a vast army of warriors.

King Sagara, pleased with his good fortune, now planned a great yagna and Asvamedha which would not only extend his kingdom but take over the powers of even Lord Indra, the king of gods. Sagara sent Anshuman with a pure white horse into the neighbouring kingdoms. Wherever the horse went the countries became Sagara's because no king wanted to wage war with him. Soon Indra in heaven, worried as the horse began to get closer to his territory, decided to steal the horse and hide it in some safe place where none could find it.

Sagara was furious at this and sent his sixty thousand sons to search for the white horse. They looked everywhere but were not able to find it. Then they began to dig into the earth to reach the lower regions. But as they dug deeper and deeper, the gods began to get alarmed at their destructive work, fearing they would destroy the earth, and appealed to Brahma. The lord assured them that Vishnu would protect his bride, the earth, and halt the march of these sixty thousand sons of Sagara. So when they reached the core of the earth and found their horse standing near a sage who was meditating, the sons cried out in triumph. But before they could do anything, they were burnt to ashes by the sage Kapila who was actually Lord Vishnu in another form.

When Sagara could not find any trace of either his sacrificial horse or his sixty thousand sons, he sent his eldest son to look for them. Anshuman, after searching the entire world, finally reached the underground world where the ashes of his brothers lay scattered. Shocked and overwhelmed with grief, he broke down and began to cry. Just then Garuda appeared and consoled him with these words, 'Grieve not, O hero, for their death was ordained. The only way you can redeem their sins and set their spirits free is to get the holy river Ganga down to earth. It will not be an easy task and you must do severe penance for many hundred years to convince the gods to send their beloved Ganga down from heaven. But only her purifying waters can save your kinsmen from their terrible fate.'

The prince took the horse, but King Sagara was so disconsolate that, though he tried, he could not think of a way to bring Ganga down to earth. After his death, Anshuman too failed to liberate his brothers and finally this difficult task was left to his grandson, Bhagirath. In order to accomplish this, Bhagirath, who had no sons, decided to do severe penance for many thousand years in the hope that the gods would help him liberate his ancestors and also grant him a son and heir. Finally Brahma, pleased with his devotion, appeared before him and asked him what he desired. Bhagirath requested the god to send Ganga down to set his ancestors free and also asked for a son. Brahma agreed to grant him his wish but warned him that it may not be possible to hold Ganga when she descends. To solve this problem, the lord of creation gave Bhagirath this advice: 'I shall grant you your wish since you deserve it. I will order the heavenly Ganga to descend to the earth. But who will hold her torrent, which is like the force of a million charging horses? Ganga's waves will shatter the earth with the power of her current. Only a god can bear her force and not just any god but the lord of destruction. Shiva alone has the power to bear her descent. Try and win his favour if you can. Pray to him, O prince, since he is easily pleased and will surely grant you your wish.' Saying this Brahma returned to heaven, but Bhagirath remained standing in one place with his arms raised for an entire year till Shiva appeared before him and promised to hold Ganga when she descended to the earth.

Now Ganga was not at all pleased when she was told to go and flow on earth. 'No one asked me while all these plans were being made. Why should I go and liberate these sixty thousand humans? I am quite happy here in heaven and have no wish to descend to earth,' she said, tossing her beautiful head. But when Brahma commanded her she had no choice but to obey. As she prepared to descend, she hissed angrily to herself, 'With my flood I shall sweep him and whirl him into the deepest pool under the earth.'

Ganga made plans to fall from heaven with such fury that Shiva would never be able to contain her. That is how she would get her revenge, she thought, gathering her waves around her like a warrior preparing for battle. But Shiva, who knew what was happening in all three worlds, read her mind and laughed. 'Let her try whatever tricks she wants. I know how to subdue her,' he said. Then Ganga began to pour down from the heavens in such a rage that even the gods trembled. Her waters churning around like a whirlpool, her waves crashed out of the skies, ready to shatter the earth. As she got closer and was about to flood him with her torrent, Shiva looked up and smiled. Then he shut his three eyes and caught her in his hair. There he held her effortlessly like an eagle holds a sparrow. Ganga, surprised and even more angry now, twisted and turned, swirled around furiously but she could not set herself free, Shiva held her in the coils of his matted locks till gradually her anger abated. Then, made humble by Shiva's touch, Ganga flowed out as a gentle as a newborn calf. Her waves flowed into the sacred Vindu lake, from where she made her way into seven streams. One branch began to follow Bhagirath as he made his way to the place where his ancestors lay buried.

People of the earth rejoiced as they saw the heavenly Ganga following the king and came out to worship her with flowers and fruits.

But on the way Ganga made the mistake of flooding the sacrificial flame of a sage named Jahnu. In his anger, he drank up all the water and suddenly Bhagirath saw all his efforts coming to nothing. He again prayed to Brahma who came to his rescue, asking the sage to release Ganga. Jahnu agreed to do so but allowed Ganga to flow out of his ears. From then on one of Ganga's names became Jahnavi, or the daughter of Jahnu. Finally Bhagirath reached the ocean, and descended to the depths along with Ganga. They reached the place where the ashes of the sixty thousand sons of Sagara were lying and, as soon as Ganga touched them with her sparkling waters, the spirits of all the dead kinsmen of Bhagirath were set free. Purified by her waves, one by one they rose into the sky and made their way to heaven.

The Mahabharata unfolds its saga with King Shantanu falling in love with the heavenly maiden Ganga. This legend from the Adi Parva tells us how she became the wife of Shantanu and the mother of Bhishma—the grandsire and one of the most important heroes in the Mahabharata.

Once, while hunting on the banks of the river, King Shantanu saw a beautiful young woman. Mesmerized by her exquisite heavenly form, the king wanted to marry her at once. Forgetting everything, he offered her his love, his kingdom, his wealth and his life. Ganga was silent for a while and then when the infatuated king beseeched her over and over again, she agreed to be his wife. 'O noble king, I shall become your wife but only on certain conditions. You must never ask me who I am or where I have come from. You must never stand in the way of whatever I do, whether good or bad, right or wrong. You must never be angry with me on any account, however provoked you may be, or say anything that displeases me. Only if you agree to all these conditions, will I marry you but if you ever break any of these vows I shall leave you at once.' King Shantanu, deeply in love with her, agreed and they were married at once.

They lived a life of perfect happiness and bliss, unaware of the world around them. Then one day, much to Shantanu's joy, Ganga gave birth to a child. But his happiness turned to horror when Ganga took the newborn baby and cast him into the river. She returned home smiling gently, and, King Shantanu, though distraught, could not break his promise to question her. Ganga had seven sons by Shantanu and each one she cast away in the river. King Shantanu's heart was filled with despair. 'Who is my beautiful wife? Where has she come from? Is she a witch or a heavenly form?' he wondered but dared not ask. 'Why did she drown her babies in the river?'

Shantanu watched his sons die one by one, and though he was crazed with grief, he did not break his promise to Ganga because he still loved her. He did not question her behaviour nor did he blame her for murdering his children. In silent anguish, he watched her take the newborn babies to the river and drown them. When she returned she always had a happy smile on her face as if she had accomplished something wonderful. Then after she had killed seven of his sons and was about to drown the eighth son, Shantanu's resolve broke. He followed her to the river and just when she was lifting the baby to throw him into the river, he stopped her. 'Pray do not drown this son of mine,' he cried, knowing he had broken his promise. Ganga turned to him in anger and said, 'O king, you have broken your word to me. You said you would not question anything I did however wrong it seemed. But love for your son made you forget your promise. Now I shall have to leave you but before I go let me tell you why I did these deeds which seemed wrong to you.' Then Ganga began to narrate the story of the Astavasus to Shantanu.

One day, while roaming in the forest, one of the Astavasus, Dyau, saw the divine cow Nandini which belonged to sage Vasishtha. Dyau recalled that his wife had wanted this heavenly cow which gave milk all the time, so he asked his brothers to help him steal her. When the sage returned to his hermitage and found that Nandini was missing, he flew into a rage. With his divine powers he got to know at once that the Astavasus had stolen her, so he cursed them. 'All you eight Astavasus who have done this wicked deed will be born on earth as humans.' The Astavasus came rushing to Vasishtha and fell at his feet. 'Please forgive us, we have committed a great sin. O sage, we return Nandini to you. Please do not curse us to be born as humans just for our one mistake,' they cried. Sage Vasishtha's anger had subsided when he saw his beloved cow Nandini, so he changed the curse. 'You shall be born as humans but you will die and return to heaven at once. But you—Dyau—you were the one responsible for the theft. You will have to live on earth for a longer period.' As the Astavasus set out on their journey to the earth they met Ganga, who agreed to help them by becoming their mother on earth.

'That is why I had to drown our sons, who were the Astavasus, in the river one by one. This child who remains is Dyau. I shall bring him up and return him to you as my gift,' said Ganga and disappeared with the child.

Many years passed as King Shantanu ruled his kingdom in a wise and benevolent way. Then one day he was wandering along the banks of the Ganga when he saw a beautiful boy. To his amazement, the king saw that the little boy was amusing himself by casting a dam made of arrows across the raging river. The beautiful form of goddess Ganga suddenly appeared in the middle of the river and spoke to the king. 'This is Devavrata, the eighth son who I took with me. He has mastered every skill of archery, learnt the Vedas from Vasishtha. Take this son of ours, who will be a great hero.' Ganga gave the boy, who was covered with gold ornaments, to King Shantanu. Then she blessed them and went back to heaven. Devavrata later became the great hero Bhishma of the Mahabharata.

Kali

Her outstretched tongue distinguishes her from all other goddesses in the Hindu pantheon. Her nakedness, unbound hair, association with blood and gore, and unbridled sexuality challenge conventional ideas of divinity. So much so that, to the uninformed eye Kali appears less as a manifestation of the divine, and more as a bloodthirsty ogress—a patron of thugs and sorcerers.

In the quest to understand Kali, it is essential to appreciate the Hindu concept of the divine. Hindus visualize the divine in various forms—human, animal, plant and mineral. Each form, with its respective narrative and rituals, serves as a gateway to realizing the ultimate unmanifest godhead. Worshippers of Shiva and Vishnu, the two most popular male manifestations of the divine, believe that the male form of the divine represents spiritual reality, while the female form symbolizes material reality. Goddess worshippers, however, associate both material and spiritual realities with the female form. To them, Kali is both Goddess or Devi (the female divinity, the supreme manifestation of the divine) and goddess (one of the several incarnations of Devi). As 'Goddess' Kali embodies both spiritual and material realities, the totality of nature, as she creates, sustains and destroys the world. As 'goddess' Kali represents only that aspect of material reality, which is wild and untamed, she complements Gauri, the radiant and gentle goddess who represents the domesticated and tamed manifestation of nature.

Worship of the Goddess in India is as ancient as civilization itself, and has its roots in the belief that the earth is a living being that nourishes all animate objects.

Kali is but one of the many goddesses of India, though undoubtedly the most popular. Despite her popularity, Kali remains an enigma to most people, including Hindus.

The form of Kali and its constituent symbols are meant to evoke bhaya and vibhitsa—fear and revulsion—forcing the observer to acknowledge the dark and unpleasant aspects of the cosmos—and hence of the divine—that one often tries to deny, repress or suppress.

Every description of Kali, after giving allowances to regional and temporal variations, has certain commonalities. She is invariably dark, naked and with unbound and dishevelled hair. She stands on Shiva's chest, holds in her hands a bloodstained scythe and a human head, has a garland of male heads around her neck and a girdle of hands around her waist. Her tongue is outstretched and smeared with blood. Surrounded by corpses, dogs and jackals, her stance looks threatening. There is no denying the fact that Kali makes an impact on the observer.

Outstretched tongue

There are many goddesses who like Kali are naked and associated with blood and death. These include Chandi, Chamunda, Bhairavi and Bhagavati. But what distinguishes Kali from other goddesses is her outstretched tongue. In some narratives, Kali spreads her tongue to drink the blood of the demon Raktabija before it touches the ground and sprouts Raktabija clones. In other narratives, Kali sticks out her tongue in embarrassment on realizing that she has stepped on her own husband in her bloodlust. In Kali temples, the tongue is smeared with the blood of sacrificed animals. With the outstretched tongue, Kali teases and mocks her devotees—she sees through their social façade and knows the dark desires they try so hard to deny or suppress. She provokes them to delve into their subconscious and confront all those memories and thoughts that they shy away from.

In many parts of India, the image of Kali does not have the characteristic outstretched tongue, though she may have fangs protruding from the corners of her mouth. This form is called Bhadra-Kali, or the 'decent Kali' who does not reject feminine grace totally. She resides in household shrines and serves as the guardian of the family.

Dark complexion

The word kali means 'black'. Kali is associated with all things black—her skin is dark, her hair black, her priests wear black, she is worshipped on new moon 'black' nights, and she is often portrayed in the company of black cats. She defies all that a fair complexion stands for—domestication, gentleness and beauty. The Goddess, or Devi, sheds her dark Kali form and becomes Gauri, who is gaur or fair, only when asked to marry Shiva.

Artists often paint Kali not black but purple or blue. Generally, the black Kali is called Smashana-Kali and enshrined in crematoria, while the blue or purple Kali is called Bhadra-Kali or Dakshina-Kali and worshipped in household and community shrines. Purple, blue or black, Kali refuses to endorse traditional concepts of beauty and auspiciousness.

Unbound hair

In traditional Hindu families, the unmarried virgin plaits her hair, the married woman oils, combs, parts and knots her hair, while the widow is made to shave her hair. Hair is thus a metaphor for sexuality—poised for fulfilment in the virgin, domesticated and controlled in the married woman, and stripped away in the widow. Kali's hair is dishevelled and unbound, indicating that her sexuality is unfettered by social norms. She represents the wild, untamed aspects of the forest—a site where sex and violence are unbridled, governed primarily by the quest for survival.

In narratives, Devi always unbinds her hair when angry or upset, or when she is called to battle. In the Tantrik Mahabharata, the untying of Draupadi's hair by the Kauravas marks the collapse of civilized conduct. Things are restored when Draupadi ties her hair after washing it with Kaurava blood after the carnage on the battlefield of Kurukshetra.

Garland of heads, girdle of arms

Kali wears around her neck a garland of human heads. These are invariably those of men, moustached and virile-looking. In one Telugu folk tradition, the heads around Kali's neck belong to a demon who had received the boon that no sooner did any of his heads touch the ground than the world would burst into flames. By placing the heads of this demon on her body Kali protects the world from destruction. The heads also represent men who have been sacrificed to her or who have sacrificed themselves to her. According to metaphysicians, the heads are symbols of the ego that must be offered to Kali by those seeking liberation from worldly ties. In the nationalistic discourse that saw Kali as Bharat Mata, these are the heads of martyrs. In the

Tantrik tradition, each head represents a Sanskrit alphabet. Kali decapitates words so that the seeker of truth is liberated from the limitations imposed by language.

Kali also has a girdle of arms around her waist, probably a later-day addition by artists who found the nakedness of Kali too discomfiting. Metaphysicians view this as the bonds of karma that Kali cuts down, liberating her devotees from the cycle of rebirth. Nationalists saw them as the arms of those who laid their lives fighting for the liberation of the motherland.

The corpses of newborns serve as Kali's earrings. Kali thus becomes the explanation for the inexplicable deaths of newborns.

Nakedness

Kali is naked. Her nakedness represents Nature, unfettered by the norms of culture. Over the centuries, as Kali moved from the periphery of spiritual practices to the centre stage, from occult rituals to household ceremonies, artists have expressed their alarm at her immodesty in various ways. Most make sure that her hair and the garland of human heads and hands cover her sexual organs. Some have even bedecked her with ornaments of pearl and gold. In temples, one often finds her naked body adorned with a silk sari. The traditional offering in Devi shrines is a piece of cloth so that she can cover her nakedness and appear as a loving bride or a nourishing mother. Through this ritual the devotee expresses his desire to see the world not as a wild and untamed place but as a place where all emotions and actions are controlled by the law of civilization. The devotee seeks not the untamed forest but the domesticated field, he wants Devi not as the bloodthirsty Kali but as the milk-giving Gauri. The disrobing of Draupadi by the Kauravas in the Mahabharata is seen in the Tantrik tradition as an attempt to unravel the codes of civilization and the return of Devi into her wild, bloodthirsty state.

Body

In her earliest descriptions in the Puranas, Kali is described as gaunt with shrivelled breasts and sunken stomach or a potbelly. Later, especially in the Tantras, and with the rise of devotional movements, Kali came to be described as an extremely beautiful girl with full breasts and a narrow waist. In the former, no attempt is made to appeal to aesthetics of the observer. In the latter, the observer is expected to reconcile the gentleness of Kali's body with the brutality of her deeds.

Although Kali is considered the consort of Shiva and in many images is shown copulating with him, she is also, like most other goddesses, called the virgin. The idea of being a virgin indicates that the Devi, the ultimate Goddess, is subservient to no man. Nature is the supreme power, shedding and reclaiming its fertility at its own volition.

Four hands

In keeping with the Hindu tradition of depicting gods and goddesses with more heads and hands than ordinary human beings, Kali is shown in most works of art with four hands. Depending on the scripture and the form of Kali being worshipped, the hands bear a variety of weapons, including scimitar, sickle, scythe, sword, axe, trident or whip. The goddess also holds in one of her hands a freshly cut male head. The blood dripping from the severed neck is collected in a cup (usually the cranium of a skull). Some scriptures say that the cup contains wine, others say it contains the nectar of immortality. In household shrines, especially where Kali is called Dakshina-Kali or Bhadra-Kali, her hands take up the postures associated with protection and blessing known as abhaya mudra and varada mudra. Kali never holds in her hands symbols associated with fertility and fructification, such as sugarcane, parrot, flowers, conch shell and pot. These are associated with the benign and motherly aspect of Devi.

Posture

In most images, Kali appears to be walking from the south in the direction of the devotee, frozen momentarily when she accidentally steps on Shiva, with her left foot on his chest. Left is associated with feminine instinct while right is the side of masculine logic. Shiva thus restrains Kali's instinctive urge to be wild and free. Narratives inform us that this is essential for the sake of safeguarding culture. Otherwise, after killing demons and drinking their blood, Kali loses all control and kills randomly until Shiva intervenes.

In Tantrik texts, Shiva is not simply a physical obstacle. He waylays Kali with his handsome face and beautiful body, stirring her erotic urges until they overpower her violent side. Hence in Tantrik iconography, Kali does not merely sit on Shiva; she copulates with him while drinking blood from a human skull.

Sometimes Kali is depicted seated on a throne held up by male gods such as Indra, Brahma, Vishnu and Shiva. As Chamunda, she sits on a pile of corpses.

Surroundings

Kali always stands amidst death and decay. It is grey and gloomy around her. She is to be found in battlegrounds and cremation grounds. The battleground witnesses the collapse of culture and orderly conduct, giving way to unbridled violence as man lets loose his rage. The cremation ground witnesses the triumph of nature as death claims one and all.

Companions

Kali's male companions include Virabhadra or the eight Bhairavas who are the fierce manifestations of Shiva. They are variously described as her sons, husbands, brothers, priests and attendants. Kali is visualized either dancing with them, being adored by them, or standing or sitting on them.

Kali's female companions include hags (dakinis), witches (yoginis), mothers (matrikas) and virgins (kumaris). Either she is part of their collective or they stand around adoring her.

Cats are sacred to the Devi in general and Kali in particular. The Devi rides, hence domesticates, male cats. Harming female cats is supposed to incur her wrath. Male cats are known to kill their young so that the female cats stop nursing, come into heat rapidly and become receptive to their sexual demands. Female cats, on the other hand, protect their young fiercely, thus becoming the symbol of motherhood. In the Devi Bhagvatam Purana and the Devi Bhagvatam, Kali rides into battle on a lion. She thus domesticates even the lord of the jungle. In Punjab, Kali is sometimes addressed as Sheravali—she of the tigers. In Tantrik art, black cats are closely associated with Kali. Occasionally, Kali is visualized riding, hence taming, a sexually aroused bull-elephant, otherwise considered to be unstoppable and dangerous. Thus Kali subdues even the most powerful beast's desire to dominate and have its way.

Kali also rides dogs, considered inauspicious, as they symbolize death. In the form of the gaunt Chamunda, Kali is associated with scorpions that have no utility, only a venomous sting and a legacy of ripping open their mothers' bellies during birth. They are all dear to Kali. In Kali's presence, even the most unappealing aspects of the cosmos reclaim their divinity.

All fertility goddesses, including Kali, are associated with snakes. Snakes are symbols of renewal—they shed their skin regularly and rejuvenate themselves just like the earth restores its fertility each year. Snakes are also symbols of kundalini, the seed of occult wisdom that lies coiled in all beings, waiting to be aroused by various Tantrik practices.

The Manifestations

Although today Kali is worshipped as an autonomous goddess manifesting in a variety of forms, in her long history she has been visualized as part of a divine female collective, as the embodiment of one of the three Devi powers, and as the 'other' face of the two-faced village-goddess. Over the centuries there has been a rise of several deities who display Kali-like characteristics but distinguish themselves from her in name and narrative. Much of the information about the manifestations of Kali comes to us from folklore and from the manuscripts known as Tantras, written after the sixth century AD.

One who takes many forms

According to Mahanirvana Tantra, Kali is adya, the primal form of the Devi, and the maha-vidyas are her emanations. Naradapancharatra mentions there are seven crore maha-vidyas and as many upa-vidyas; their number can never be settled conclusively. Thus Kali has innumerable forms and is known by many names. In the Shakti-sangama Tantra, according to Hadimata, one of the several contributors to the manuscript, Maha-Shakti is called Kali in Kerala, Tripura in Kashmir and Tara in Gauda (Bengal), while according to Kadimata, another contributor, she is called Tripura in Kerala, Tarini in Kashmira and Kali in Gaura. Kali has eight forms in Todala-Tantra: Dakshina-, Siddha-, Guhya-, Shri-, Bhadra-, Chamunda-, Smashana- and Maha-Kali. Mahakala Samhita enumerates nine types of Kali: Dakshina-, Bhadra-, Smashana-, Kala-, Guhya-, Kamakala-, Dhana-, Siddhi- and Chandika-Kali. The tenth-century Jayadhratayamala mentions twelve forms of Kali—Kalika, Dambara, Raksha, Indivara, Dhanda, Ramani, Ishana, Jiva, Virya, Dhyana, Prajna and Saptarna—each representing a state of consciousness, with the highest state symbolized by the thirteenth Kali, Kalasamkarshini.

Dakshina-Kali, enshrined in temples and even in households, is the most important of Kali's forms because it is her most acceptable and conventional form. She is characterized by a fierce but smiling face, four hands, untied hair and a garland of severed heads. She is naked, dark, full breasted, holds a severed head in one hand and a sword in the other. The third hand is raised to protect while the fourth arm blesses. She steps on a corpse-like Shiva as she approaches from the south. The devotee considers her his mother.

Smashana-Kali is the form of Kali that is restricted to the cremation ground. Unlike Dakshina-Kali who is bluish purple in colour, she is black. She neither blesses, nor gives boons. She looks fierce with snakes slithering around her body and jackals keeping her company. She drinks blood, yells into the night and dances with goblins. The Tantrik aspirant seeks to face her without fear and thus win her appreciation.

Siddha-Kali is the form taken by Kali when she is pleased with the Tantrik aspirant. In this form, she reveals the occult mysteries of the cosmos to the worthy hero and makes him powerful. Bejewelled with the sun and moon as her earrings, she has the complexion of a deep blue lotus in the moonlight. She has a flaming tongue and drinks the nectar of immortality from a skull, which she shares with the Tantrik hero.

Guhya-Kali, according to Tantra Sara, is the mysterious occult teacher of Tantra who lives in caves far away from human habitation. She has sunken eyes, wears black clothes, and has snakes for jewellery. Sometimes she has the crescent moon on her forehead, sometimes she nurses Shiva who takes the form of her child, and sometimes she appears with ten heads before those determined to see her.

As Bhadra-Kali, the fierce protector, she holds weapons of war in her hands, including an axe, a trident, a whip, a bell and a rattle-drum to frighten enemies. The skull that she uses as her drinking bowl also serves as the top of her mace.

As Chamunda-Kali, she is dark, emaciated, gaunt with bloodshot eyes, fangs and claws, shrivelled breasts, a scorpion on her sunken belly and a tiger skin around her waist. She sits on a pile of corpses, eats entrails, smears herself with gore, and drinks blood.

One of two

Traditionally, Tantrik schools are classified as Kali-kula and Shri-kula—the former worships the dark, fearsome forms of the Devi and the latter worships the fair, alluring forms. As Kali, the Devi is Tripura-Bhairavi, the most terrifying form in the three worlds; as Shri-Vidya, she is Tripura-Sundari, the most beautiful form. As Kali, the Devi bears weapons of war and skulls; as Shri, she bears symbols of fertility, including sugarcane, a parrot, conch shells and lotus flowers. As Kali, the Devi demands blood sacrifice; as Shri she gives food and knowledge to her devotees. Kali thus represents the 'other' face of Nature, one that is wild and untamed, one that is associated with death and decay, one that mankind tries very hard to deny, repress and suppress. Those of the Kali-kula school are also known as Vama-Tantriks or the left-handed Tantriks because their rites include objects and activities that defile the sanctity of religion, such as the use of flesh, alcohol, blood, corpses, hallucinogens and sex. Those of the Dakshina-Tantra or the right-handed Tantra school, who worship the Devi as Shri-Vidya, practise the same rites symbolically, substituting fruits and vegetables for animal and human sacrifices and red powder for blood.

The idea of the 'two-faced' goddess is at the core of the simplest and most ancient form of Devi-worship that exists in most villages of India, where a grama-devi or a village-goddess embodies the village itself. The deity is commonly represented by a vermillion- or saffron-smeared stone with a prominent pair of metal eyes. She has no body; the entire village—with its houses and fields—constitutes her body. The villagers in effect, live on the body of the village-goddess. This body is nothing but the wilderness, which has been fenced and domesticated to sustain a human settlement. Metaphorically speaking, wild Nature has been tamed, Kali has been converted to Shri, in order to establish and sustain the village.

However, once a year, the village-goddess returns to her wild state: Shri becomes Kali. Her tongue spreads across the village and she demands blood. This happens in autumn, after the harvest. This is the time when a male buffalo representing the dark, unspoken desires of the villagers—visualized as a demon—is sacrificed to the village-goddess. In the celebrations that follow, women get hysterical fits as they let their suppressed emotions express themselves. Men walk on fire or indulge in hook-swinging. Blood is spilt and pain experienced. The village experiences the wild side of Nature that the villagers otherwise keep at bay with their rules in order to establish and preserve the community.

Villagers address the grama-devi as Amma, Ai, Mata—various vernacular terms for mother. Her life-giving form Shri is known by various names, including Gauri, the radiant one; Mangala, the auspicious one; Bimala, the untainted one; and Lalita, the beautiful one. Her life-taking form Kali is known as Bhairavi, the fearsome one; Chamunda, the killer; Chandi, the aggressive one; and Jari-Mari, the hot-cold one. The following story from Shiva Purana clearly links the two forms of the Devi:

Kali's dark form, outstretched tongue, naked body scared everyone in the three worlds. The terrified gods, demons and humans invoked Shiva and begged him to calm her down. Shiva promised to help. He stood before Kali and began laughing. 'Why are you laughing?' asked a curious Kali. 'They say you are beautiful. But take a look at yourself; you look dark and hideous,' replied Shiva. Kali went to a river and saw her reflection. She realized what Shiva said was true. She bathed in the river until her black skin turned golden. She emerged looking beautiful. Shiva called her Gauri, the radiant one, and took her to his abode where she resumed her role as his consort. Kali's dark complexion was absorbed by the river, which became deep blue in colour. The river became known as Kalindi.

One of three

Between the fifth century BC and the fifth century AD, Hinduism was transformed. Vedic rituals were being abandoned, monastic ideology was gaining popularity and society was becoming increasingly theistic. People sought an almighty deity who answered their prayers and solved their problems. Some visualized the deity as male—either the ascetic Shiva or the regal Vishnu. Others visualized the deity as female.

Devi-worshippers were known as Shaktas. Their deity, Mahadevi (which literally means 'the great goddess') was the embodiment of shakti (energy or substance of the cosmos), prakriti (the natural, material world), and maya (perceived reality). In shrines, she was represented by three stones, each stone embodying a third of her divinity. The stones represented Maha-Lakshmi, Maha-Saraswati, and Maha-Kali, the goddesses of wealth, knowledge and power. Shrines where three stones still represent the Devi are located at Vaishno-Devi in Jammu, Mookambika in Karnataka and Maha-Lakshmi in Mumbai.

As one of the triad, Kali is rarely depicted with an outstretched tongue, but her symbols such as the lion and the trident dominate the shrine. Blood sacrifice associated with Kali is, however, discouraged as worshippers prefer to visualize the goddess in her milder, vegetarian form.

The following story from a Kannada ballad, which is a recurring theme in many folk narratives, informs us how the three forms of the Devi came into being when male deities usurped the primal position once occupied by the ultimate female divinity. In the story, cultural values such as incest taboo are associated with the male deities, implying that the female deities are embodiments of 'wild Nature' while the male deities are upholders of 'domesticated Culture':

Once long ago, even before there was the sun and the moon in the sky, there bloomed a lotus in the ocean of milk. On that lotus sat the Goddess, Mahadevi, who is Adi-Maya-Shakti, the mother of all forms. All alone and lonely, she decided to create a consort to please her. She produced three eggs. From the first one came Brahma, who looked like a priest ready to perform a *yagna*. From the second came Vishnu, who looked like a king ready to uphold dharma. From the third came Shiva, with matted locks, who looked like an ascetic. All three were handsome and the Devi desired them all. She first went to Brahma. 'Be my husband and make me happy,' she said, smiling coquettishly. Brahma was horrified. 'You are my mother,' he said, 'You ask me to do what a son must not do!' Mahadevi said, 'This does not apply to me. I make the rules.' Brahma refused to satisfy the Devi. Angry, she opened her third eye, let loose a glance of fire and reduced Brahma to ashes. The

Devi then approached Vishnu. He too turned away, refusing to do what a son must not do with his mother. His fate was the same as Brahma's. Then standing between two piles of ashes where Brahma and Vishnu once stood, Mahadevi looked at Shiva. 'Well, will you be my husband and quench my thirst?' Shiva knew what was in store for him if he refused. 'I will,' he said, 'But don't you think to be a worthy husband I should have more strength than you? Otherwise everyone will mock you and me.' The Devi agreed. She shared her wisdom with Shiva, even the ability to create things out of thin air. But Shiva was not satisfied. Give me the jewel that rests on your forehead. 'That is no jewel. That is the third eye, the source of all my power,' said Mahadevi. 'Give me the third eye, then,' said Shiva. Mahadevi, blinded by lust, agreed. She plucked out her third eye and gave it to Shiva. No sooner had he laid his hands on the Devi's power than he reduced her to ashes. Then using his new-found powers, Shiva revived Brahma and Vishnu. They looked at the heap of ash where Mahadevi once stood. 'What do we do with that?' They decided to create wives out of it. They divided the ash into three heaps. Brahma transformed one heap into Lakshmi, made her the goddess of wealth, called her his sister and gave her in marriage to Vishnu. Vishnu transformed the second heap into Kali, made her the goddess of power, called her his sister and gave her in marriage to Shiva. Shiva transformed the third heap into Saraswati, made her the goddess of knowledge, called her his sister and gave her in marriage to Brahma. From the tiny amounts of ash left behind came many dark, naked and fierce-looking goddesses with fangs, bloodshot eyes and unbound hair, holding serpents and sickles in their hands. These became village-goddesses, ready to fight with demons and inflict disease on villagers who annoyed them.

One of several

Kali or a Kali-like goddess is often one of the seven kumaris (virgins), one of the seven matrikas (mothers), one of the ten maha-vidyas (teachers), one of the sixty-four yoginis (witches) or one of the 108 dakinis (crones). Although each member of these groups has a unique name and a characteristic form, no member is worshipped in isolation. They are sacred as a group.

The matrikas are no different from kumaris—virgins who inadvertently become the mothers of Skanda, the hypermasculine commander of the celestial armies. Skanda is born of the seed of one god—Agni, the fire-god, in early scriptures, and Shiva, the ascetic-god, in later scriptures—which is so potent that it needs to be incubated in seven virgin wombs. The narratives vary on how the seven sisters, sometimes described as wives of the seven celestial sages, get pregnant. In the following story from the Mahabharata, the sisters make love to Agni through a surrogate:

The fire-god, Agni, burnt with lust at the sight of the wives of the seven celestial sages but he knew that his passion for married women was inappropriate. He would caress the women with his heat and light each time they approached the fire-altar to make offerings to the gods. Realizing that it was just a matter of time before Agni had illicit relations with these unsuspecting women, Agni's consort Svaha decided to take the matter into her own hands. She took the form of the seven women and made love to her husband seven times. She succeeded only six times as the seventh sister was too chaste. Agni therefore spilt his seed six times. This Svaha collected and transformed into a single hypermasculine child called Skanda who was powerful enough to lead the celestial armies even when he was a child. His passion spent, Agni thanked Svaha for saving him from committing an unforgivable crime.

In the Skanda Purana, six of them become pregnant when they bathe in a pond in which the gods have placed a potent seed of Shiva. Though innocent, the women are accused of adultery. To purify their bodies of shame, they shed the unborn child. A forest fire fuses the six foetuses into the six-headed Skanda. The virgins are sometimes called the Krittikas, hence Skanda is also known as Kartika, the son of the six virgins.

The Mahabharata mentions that outraged at being penalized for no fault of theirs, the virgins turn into ferocious beings. They decide to kill Skanda, but no sooner do they lay their eyes on their child than they are overcome with maternal affection. Skanda declares, 'If women do not worship you, feel free to destroy their unborn and newborn children.' The virgins thus became goddesses of several childhood ailments. They are appeased with offerings of neem leaves, curd and lemons every time a child or pregnant woman has fever with pox or rashes. Their shrines are no more than seven vermillion-smeared stones on the banks of water bodies, usually under neem trees.

In later sculptures, written after the tenth century AD, the seven mothers are visualized as the female forms of seven popular Hindu gods: Shiva, Vishnu, Brahma, Narasimha, Varaha, Kumara and Indra. Sometimes, the goddess Chamunda is listed amongst them. Chamunda with her gaunt features, nakedness and bloodlust is said to be a form of Kali.

Like the matrikas, the maha-vidyas and the yoginis too appear in narratives as manifestations of outrage. Some of them have the form of Kali. The maha-vidyas first appear when Sati decides to disrupt her father's yagna, intended to insult her hermit-husband Shiva. The yoginis appear when Parvati threatens to destroy the world unless her son Vinayaka, who has been beheaded by Shiva, is restored to life.

A careful observation of these groups shows that they signify the various reactions Nature has evoked in man. Nature can be anything from the wild and terrifying to the tame and beautiful. Kali embodies the wild side with her nakedness and bloodlust, while Kamala embodies the gentle side with her bejewelled form and lotus seat. Often these collective goddesses have one male form beside them, either Skanda or Ganesha, or more commonly, Bhairava— the fierce form of Shiva. The male form is described variously as the attendant, priest, brother, son or consort of the divine female collective.

Almost Kali

Across India we find many Kali-like goddesses. Prominent among these are Chamunda, Alakshmi, Bhagavati,

Chinnamastika, and Tara. They probably originated from the same primordial cultural substratum from where all forms of the Devi emerged.

Most devotees do not distinguish between Chamunda and Kali. In some scriptures Chamunda is clearly identified as a form of Kali. Their identities often coalesce because they are dark, naked, wild and bloodthirsty. But there are differences. Chamunda is emaciated and ugly while Kali is dishevelled but beautiful. Chamunda sits on a pile of corpses while Kali stands on Shiva. Unlike Kali, Chamunda does not stretch out her tongue. Chamunda rides ghosts and has scorpions on her body, while Kali rides lions, and sometimes elephants. Chamunda is associated more with death and decay while Kali is associated more with unbridled sex and violence.

Alakshmi, the goddess of misfortune, is the sister of Lakshmi, the goddess of fortune. Together they constitute the totality of the Devi. While in Tantra the inauspicious form of the Devi is worshipped, in Vaishnavism—strictly a religion of householders—preference is given only to the auspicious forms. Thus, in Vaishnava rituals, Lakshmi is worshipped as the consort of Vishnu who is the upholder of social values and worldly order, while Alakshmi is driven away as she embodies all things that threaten civilization— dirt, pollution, gluttony, sloth, greed, envy, hunger, disease and war. While Lakshmi sits bejewelled on a lotus holding a pot, Alakshmi wears torn clothes, rides a donkey and carries a broom. Lakshmi is offered sweets and kept inside the house; Alakshmi is offered lemons and chillies and thrown out of the house. The following story illustrates the conventional attitude towards Alakshmi:

Lakshmi and Alakshmi, the goddesses of fortune and misfortune respectively, once went to a merchant and asked him who was more beautiful of the two. The merchant knew the price of annoying either one. So he came up with a very clever answer. He said, 'Lakshmi is beautiful when she walks into the house while Alakshmi is beautiful when she leaves the house.' Immediately, Lakshmi walked towards the merchant's house while Alakshmi walked away from it. Consequently, the merchant was visited by fortune while misfortune stayed away, much to the merchant's delight.

Bhagavati is one of the most popular 'hot' goddesses of Kerala. In the ritual art of Teyyam, she is invoked through oracles and through the dancers who go in a trance as soon as she 'enters' their bodies and begins to 'speak' through their tongues. Usually the goddess has no permanent shrine dedicated to her. Devotees create her image on the floor using coloured powder on festival days, which is wiped out at the end of the ceremony. The goddess looks ferocious with bloodshot eyes, fangs and clawed fingers. She demands offerings, usually chickens and goats, from villagers before promising them peace and prosperity. Sometimes songs with obscene lyrics describing her insatiable sexual cravings are sung to amuse this virgin goddess, although this practice is now on the wane. In narratives it is said that this goddess was first invoked to kill a demon. Every year after this demon is ritually killed—either in song or through sacrifice—Bhagavati leaves the body of the oracle or the dancer. The devotees who invoked her return to their daily routine, safe in the knowledge that Bhagavati is happy and will take care of them until her return the following year.

Chinnamastika, like Kali, is one of the maha-vidyas—teachers of occult wisdom. Chinnamastika is described as a naked goddess who cuts her own head and drinks the blood that spurts out of her severed neck while either copulating with Shiva or dancing on a couple making love. The image brings together acts of sex, violence, defence and nourishment. Chinnamastika reconciles the creative and destructive sides of the cosmos as she feeds on what she kills. She embodies the stark reality of Nature that culture shies away from. Her image is never enshrined in households because it appeals more to the Tantrik aspirant who has broken free from the restrictions imposed by civilized society and who is willing to explore those aspects of the universe that society deems inappropriate and inauspicious.

In Bengal, Tara is another name for Kali, although the two are treated as two distinct goddesses in the list of maha-vidyas. In Tibet, Tara is the name of a goddess who is quite unlike her Bengali namesake. The Tibetan Tara is described as a gentle and charming goddess who holds a lotus in her hand. She was born from the tear of compassion shed by the Bodhisattva Avatilokeshwara when he heard the cries of those trapped in the cycle of rebirths. The link between the Tibetan Tara and the Bengali Tara has perhaps much to do with the religious communication that existed for centuries between Bengal and Tibet.

In Tibetan Tantrik Buddhism, a goddess who is more like Kali, at least in form, is Nairatma ('no soul')—the consort of Heruka. Her name means shunya or nothingness into which the Bodhichitta, the enlightened soul, merges on attaining Nirvana. That is why she is represented in eternal union with her consort.

Individually she is represented as standing in a dancing mode on a corpse. Her face looks terrible with bare and protruding tongue and she carries a kartari (dagger) in her right hand and kapala (skull-bowl) in the left, just like Kali.

For most people, the divine is associated with beauty and love. Images of gods and goddesses are therefore expected to please the eye and the heart. Kali, however, defies these expectations. She is neither beautiful nor loving; she is dark, gaunt, and bloodthirsty. Her form takes one by surprise— frightening at first, then confounding. Kali forces a re-examination of all preconceived notions associated with divinity.

Culture struggles to explain Kali. Desperate attempts are made to rationalize her as the 'killer of demons', and the 'protecting mother'. Images are created that edit out her wild sexuality. Paintings embellish her with jewellery meant for tame wives. The men she decapitates are depicted as outlaws and demons. Society does what it has always done— transforming or denying what it cannot, or does not, or will not, understand.

But Kali gives this cultural manipulation a slip. She remains a dark and wild enigma challenging the seer, the devotee, and the sorcerer, mocking all preconceived notions. She demands acceptance of all that she represents. Her form and narratives about her throw up questions: Why is she dark and naked? Why is her hair unbound? Why does she copulate openly sitting on top of her lover? Why does she drink blood? Why does she favour sorcerers? The answers force us to confront the dark secrets we shove into our subconscious.

Kali is life who feeds on life. Kali is the unbridled and impersonal sex and violence that makes the cycle of existence go round. Kali stirs the consciousness by copulating with Shiva. She is the raw primal power that existed before there were culture and society, before there were law, ethics and morality. She stands beyond the pall of prejudices, values, and judgements. She encompasses the totality of nature and of life, unfettered by social norms and cultural values.

Kali reminds us that beneath our social indoctrination fester thoughts and desires that do not conform to what is culturally appropriate. The beast within us may be tamed but if we deny its existence or repress it beyond a point, it may slip out and strike, manifesting as rape or riot. Hidden in our hearts are ideas that may not be spoken, but need, at the very least, silent acknowledgement.

Beneath the mask, beneath the self-denial and the self-discipline exists a Kali in all of us.

HANUMAN

When demons overran the world, tyrannizing mankind, Lord Vishnu came down to Earth in the form of Rama, a human. Rama was destined to live the life of an ordinary mortal, with all the attendant suffering and pain. It was when Rama's fortunes were at their lowest that Hanuman came into his life. Swami Chinmayananda writes, 'From the moment Anjaneya [Hanuman] meets with Rama, [the] Ramayana distinctly reveals a mysterious [unfolding] of great powers, an explosion of inconceivable merits and beauties.' In other words, the epic takes a new turn and becomes a saga of success and hope after Hanuman steps in.

Hanuman was born into the Vanara tribe, a clan of semi-deities, the males of which wore monkey-like tails 'as an ornament'. There are many and varied accounts given of Hanuman's birth in different sacred texts of Hinduism, but they all agree that he was endowed, even at birth, with extraordinary valour, wisdom and steadfastness. However, it was only when Rama found him, years later, that he could realize his true potential. Till he met Rama, Hanuman had been one of the highest-ranking advisors of the Vanara-king Sugriva. But Sugriva had never been able to tap Hanuman's enormous potential. Only Rama had it in him to bring out Hanuman's divine powers. In turn, Hanuman helped Rama fulfil his mission on earth; he was the ideal lieutenant: brave, intelligent, totally committed to his master, selfless and humble.

After the battle of Lanka had been won, and Rama and Sita had returned to Ayodhya, Rama's brothers, Lakshmana, Bharata and Shatrughna said to Hanuman, 'Clearly you are not a monkey. You wear the sacred thread. Your clothes and jewellery, your religious rituals and mansions in Kishkindha, they are identical to those of men. You are an expert in all the scriptures. You know all the natural sciences. Monkeys don't do all this. Then what kind of a people are you Vanaras?' 'I am an upa-devata (demi-deity),' Hanuman replied. 'I rank below the devatas (deities) but not above humans. How can I rank higher than the human form that Rama is in?'

Worshippers through the centuries have not made such subtle distinctions. To them, Hanuman is both an all-powerful god and the greatest devotee and there is no contradiction in this. Even those who maintain that Lord Rama is the goal and Hanuman the path to that goal, believe that the worship of Rama is incomplete till prayers are offered to Hanuman as well. On the other hand, when Hanuman is worshipped independently and alone, as he often is, devotees celebrate all the acts that he performed for Rama. (There are also several Shaivites who do not give Lord Rama quite the same importance as they do to Lord Shiva. They worship Hanuman as the eleventh Rudr, or aspect, of Shiva.)

To his worshippers, Hanuman epitomizes piety, duty, discipline, strength, chastity, modesty, altruism, scholarship and simplicity. He is in many ways the most reliable, the most accessible and the least controversial of all the deities of Hinduism. Above all, he is the keeper of Rama's gates. Not only does he guard the Lord's temples and home, he also controls access to Him.

The Greatest Devotee

The *Brihad-bhagvatamrit* records that the sage Narada once asked a Brahmin in Prayag (modern Allahabad), 'Who is the greatest devotee of God?'

'Ask the king,' the Brahmin said.

The king said, 'Lord Indra is a great devotee.'

However, Lord Indra himself said, 'No one is more devoted to God than Lord Brahma.'

Narada went to Lord Brahma with the same question. Brahma said, 'Shiva is a great devotee of Brahman.'

But Lord Shiva said, 'Those who live in Vaikunth [heaven] are truly devoted to Vishnu. These days Vishnu lives in Dwarka and is known as Krishna. Prahlada, who lives on earth, is his greatest worshipper.'

Prahlada was amazed by this assessment of his devotion. He said, 'Hanuman had the honour of serving Rama for many thousand years. The deities had blessed him with countless powers and gifts. There can be no greater devotee of God than he.'

In the *Srimad Bhagvat*, Sri Badarayana worshipped Hanuman and called him the 'param bhagvat' (greatest devotee) of Lord Vishnu.

To most Hindus, Hanuman is an obedient servant who is humble and gives credit for all his successes to his master.

He denies himself all pleasures, especially sensual ones. He is the Supreme Devotee whose faith never wavers. He is also known for, what Catherine Ludvik (in her book *Hanuman in the Ramayana of the Ramacaritamanasa of Tulsi Dasa)* describes as 'an obsession with propriety'.

Since at least the fourteenth century Hanuman has also been the symbol of muscular Hinduism. As a warrior he was an exceptionally good fighter, possessing great courage and intelligence, but also one who always behaved very nobly towards his opponents. By the seventeenth century other aspects of the Supreme Devotee, too, got emphasized. In Vijayanagar, for instance, he was also revered as a patron of music (with a veena in his hands) and, more importantly, as the path to the Supreme Reality. He was therefore shown sitting at Lord Rama's feet, reading a sacred book. Rama would interpret the text as the *Para Brahma Tattv,* the essence of the Supreme Being.

As a child Hanuman was an outstanding student and in his old age a great scholar, writer and composer. His grammar was always perfect. Therefore, he is also the patron deity of students, scholars and grammarians.

Above all, Hanuman is the quintessential gatekeeper. Tulasi Das wrote:

> You are the guardian of Shri Rama's gate
> No one can enter without Your mandate.

As a servant of Lord Rama, Hanuman desired nothing more than the satisfaction that came from the fact that his master had given him an opportunity to serve him.

Hanuman is thus the epitome of bhakti—devotion—and this is the basis of all his other qualities.

The Attributes and Qualities of Hanuman

Valmiki quotes Sita as telling the son of the wind, Hanuman, 'You are the embodiment of virtue, bravery, wisdom, knowledge, munificence, mercy, power, forbearance, humility and all that is good.' Nilkanth, the famous ancient Vedic expert, added, 'Hanuman is an incarnation of Rudr (Lord Shiva). He has not a trace of jealousy in him. He moves with enormous speed. He is a great spy and investigator. He is also a great communicator.' Others praise his diplomatic skills, first as the envoy of Sugriva and then that of Rama.

A well-known Sanskrit verse reminds us that Hanuman's qualities are: wisdom (buddhi), strength (balam), renown and positive fame (yash), patience (dhairya), fearlessness (nirbhayata), good health and an absence of ailments (arogata), indefatigability (ajadyam), and fluency of speech and facility of logic (vakpatutvam). Hanuman epitomizes bhakti (piety), brahmacharya (chastity), namrata (modesty), nishkam karm (altruistic deeds or altruism), seva (duty or ministration), shakti (energy), and vidya (scholarship). He also represents curiosity, intelligence and discipline.

Hanuman has complete control over all five senses. The process of keeping the senses on a tight leash is called indriya nigreh, and Hanuman, who has mastery over this process at all times, is thus also known as Jitendra. This, of course, is only to be expected from one who is 'the only perfect sanyasi (hermit or ascetic)'. The various attributes of a true hermit-saint have been discussed in Advait Vedant literature, especially in Bhashyakara Shankaracharya's works. Hanuman is the only person who satisfies all the conditions.

However, the four best-known divine attributes of Hanuman are akhand brahmacharya (undivided, uninterrupted celibacy), immense physical prowess, a mastery of the scriptures (which include grammar and the fine arts) and dasya bhakti (worship by serving the Lord). For the Achintyabhedabheda school of the Gaudiya Vaishnav Sampradaya, founded by Chaitanya Mahaprabhu, Hanuman's life itself is the best example of dasya bhakti. He made sure that everything, important or trivial, which the Lord required to be done, was performed. Besides, he did not let the Lord leave his mind even for a moment.

Incidentally, the attitude (or emotion) of actual physical service to the Lord is called das(ya) bhav. When this matures into worship it is called das(ya) bhakti. In dasya bhakti the devotee has unflinching faith in the Lord, he is completely dedicated to the Lord and he surrenders and sacrifices himself totally to the Lord. In turn he finds pure, unsullied happiness when he serves God. Hanuman said, 'The one thing that I am proud of is that I am a servant and [no less than] the lord of the Raghus is my master.'

What Hanuman Symbolizes

The Ramayana can be read at two levels: as an adventure story for children and as a string of spiritual metaphors. The latter view is accepted in Vedanta. Here, the characters of the Ramayana are seen as souls trying to travel towards the Truth (symbolized by Rama). Sita represents the jiv-atma, the soul of the mortal individual. She gets so taken in by the love of material goods (symbolized by the golden deer) that she loses track of the Truth. The ocean represents the chasm between the Truth and seekers who stray from the path. Rama represents the Truth or the Supreme God (param-atma). Devdutt Pattanaik (in his book *Hanuman: An Introduction)* has translated param-atma as 'the soul of the cosmos' which, too, the Supreme God is.

What does Hanuman represent in a metaphorical reading of the Ramayana? He brings the seeker and the Truth together. But he is not the bridge. That honour belongs to Rama alone (as Tulasi Das reminds us). Hanuman represents devotion (bhakti). His role is to serve (or help) the jiv when it is in trouble. He helps unite the jiv (Sita, or we mortals) with the Truth (Rama). The point is that Rama could not have rescued Sita (or others who are trapped in worldly desires) had Hanuman not helped her (and others) first. So, if Rama is the destination, Hanuman is the road that we have to take (and the method that we have to adopt) in order to get there. Hanuman has the capacity to help us because he serves God with his body and his heart—he is pure and his mind has evolved to the highest level possible.

Ravana is the symbol of ahankar (arrogance, the ego). Lanka, with its dazzling affluence and material goods (including aircraft and jewel-studded, gilded, multi-storeyed houses) represents corporeal pleasures. The wall that surrounds Lanka is the wall within, which are trapped those of us who are caught up with all things material. Hanuman sets fire to this array of expensive material goods. The meaning is obvious.

Of course, Sita's desire for the deer's golden fleece was brief and temporary, and she regretted it almost immediately afterwards. Which is why she was in Lanka and yet not a part of it. She chose to live in a secluded grove rather than in the comforts of the palace. Satyanarayana suggests that Hanuman burnt down golden Lanka with 'the flame of Sita's grief'. He also believes that the hill with the miracle herb, which Hanuman carried across the ocean for the wounded Lakshmana, represents 'the eternal wisdom of Vedanta', which revives those who have been rendered unconscious in their battle against lust (that is, Ravana).

The Worship of Hanuman

According to Dr R. Nagaswamy, in Valmiki's version of the story of Rama, Hanuman is fit to 'be adored and worshipped by the Indian people, on par with Lord Rama'. In Chhattisgarh, it is said, people are more devoted to Hanuman than to Rama, even though Hanuman is himself a Rama bhakt (devotee of Rama). This, obviously, is because Hanuman comes across as a friendly, accessible deity, whom anyone can approach. He stirs the emotions of the masses and has their loyalty.

All the same, it must be remembered that in Valmiki's Ramayana, Hanuman remains a Vanara, an upa-devta (demi-deity), and is not supposed to be a god. He is, in fact, more human than anything else. Clearly, Rama is always the goal and Hanuman the path to that goal. Yet, the worship of Rama is incomplete till prayers are offered to Hanuman as well. And then again, even when Hanuman is worshipped on his own, the worshipper celebrates all the acts that Hanuman performed for Rama.

The Shaivites, to whom Rama, an incarnation of Vishnu, is not as important as Shiva, worship Hanuman as the eleventh Rudr of Lord Shiva. In fact, Hanuman unites all the three major groups of Hinduism—the Shaivites, Vaishnavites and Shaktas. His idols will be found in the Vaishnavite temples of his master, Lord Rama, in shrines dedicated to Shiva, and the temples of Devi, the Mother Goddess.

Tuesday is the day associated with Hanuman in north India. However, in Maharashtra and some other parts of the country it is Saturday when attendances peak at Hanuman temples. Tuesday is the day when Rama (and, perhaps, Hanuman, too) was born. Mangal (Mars) is the planet that presides over this auspicious day. Devdutt Pattanaik writes that Saturn (Shani) and Mars are 'associated with death and war and [are] known to disrupt human life with their influence'. Since Hanuman, the friend of all nine planets, enjoys the affection of both, he is worshipped on these two days in particular.

It is said that Lord Shani is pleased when people worship Hanuman with 'sweet' oil (that is, til or sesame oil) on Saturdays. In Maharashtra, devotees offer urad daal (black gram) seeds as well. In south India worshippers place offerings of butter and garlands of vadas (also made of urad and other daals) at Hanuman's feet. In other parts of India, garlands offered to the deity are made of the flowers and leaves of arka (*Calotropis gigantean*/crown flower). Black grams (urad) with the husk removed are a popular offering even in north India.

South Indian idols of Hanuman have five heads and many arms. The *Hanumat Kavach* is recited before them. Such idols are also found in Srinagar and Jammu. The Hindi belt's favourite Hanuman prayer, of course, is the *Hanuman Chalisa*, followed by *Sankat Mochan*. In most parts of India, especially in Andhra Pradesh, the massive Sundar-kand is recited in order to request Hanuman for favours. Some communities, such as the Vallabh sampradaya (community) of the Shuddhadvait school of philosophy, pray to Rama and Hanuman for four days during the sharadiya (autumn) Navaratri. In many parts of India, Hanuman is also worshipped on his birthday.

The worship of Hanuman is a simple, uncomplicated affair. Tulasi Das, in his *Hanuman Bahuki*, writes that all that the devotee need do is praise, revere and meditate upon the son of the wind while reciting his name. Hanuman rewards all sincere devotees with whatever they ask him for. Madhavacharya of the Madhav sampradaya of Dvait philosophy wrote in the *Tantr Sara*, 'If a person prays to Hanuman he will get whatever he asks for, be it money, power, learning, or any other thing.'

What are the kinds of things that people pray to Hanuman for? Protection—from enemies, ghosts, disease, just about anything—is the most common request. Wrestlers worship the Bajrang Bali for better biceps. However, most devotees pray to Hanuman because he is the path to Rama.

The powers and munificence of Hanuman are limitless. So it is unsurprising that to his worshippers he is the ultimate protector. He is:

Sankat Mochan: When they find themselves in any kind of trouble, people worship Hanuman, who is sankat mochan (the distress remover). Hanuman's entire life, as we have seen, was dedicated to helping Rama, Sita, Sugriva, and the Vanars. He also killed evil creatures who harassed the innocent. He continues to protect all true devotees from later-day demons.

A friend of the planets: Almost all practising Hindus believe that nine stars and planets influence the lives of people. Some planets and stars (especially Shani, or Saturn) are dreaded because they are said to bring bad luck. Hanuman befriended Shani and freed the other planets from Ravana's prison. As a result he enjoys the goodwill of all nine. Hanuman's devotees pray to him for protection from the wrath of the 'negative' planets. A woman called Panvati personifies bad luck that certain planets bring. In some parts of India, idols of Hanuman show him crushing this woman under his feet. In the Bengali Ramayana, Hanuman is portrayed as an astrologer. Indeed, most Hindus believe that he is the very inventor of the science of astrology.

An enemy of ghosts and black magic: All devotees of Hanuman (also called Mahabir) know that,

> Ghosts and goblins fly away in fear
> When Mahabir, the name, they hear.

Hanuman was also given the responsibility of protecting devotees from evil spirits and black magic unleashed on them by their enemies. However, some Tantriks (Tantriks are mystics; some of them practise black magic) see Hanuman as the ultimate source of occult practices—and certain forms of black magic. This is not the mainstream Hindu view, but it is interesting that the same deity is both the fountainhead of and antidote to black magic. The Tantriks believe that Hanuman obtained his enormous supernatural powers because he was a strict celibate, in body as well as mind.

One who cures the ill: Hanuman helped bring Lakshmana—and several others—back to life. Therefore, when people meet with terrible accidents or are very ill, their friends and relatives pray to Hanuman to help the patient recover. For the same reason, most doctors trained in the ancient Indian system of medicine consider him their patron deity.

The patron deity of wrestlers and acrobats: Hanuman, the celibate god of immense strength who was born with a loincloth, is the patron deity of body builders and wrestlers. Several tribes of wandering performers, especially the Nats and the Badis of Haryana, are devotees of Hanuman.

The patron of new wells: Whenever a new well is being dug, a little temple of Hanuman is set up nearby. His protection is sought for the construction workers, and his blessings for the quality of the water.

Liberator from insects and germs: Several sects perform mystic rituals in honour of Hanuman to ensure that the insects and germs that trouble them are killed. Those who have been bitten by snakes, scorpions and other poisonous animals also pray to Hanuman to eliminate the poison. Hanuman also gives his devotees protection against epidemics and other natural disasters.

One who grants supernatural powers: In the *Hanuman Chalisa*, Tulasi Das has written about Hanuman:

> You grant the Nine Treasures and Perfections Eight
> Because Mother Janaki gave You this trait.

(The eight perfections or siddhis are actually eight supernatural powers. It was Sita—also known as Janaki—who gave Hanuman the power to bestow these on his devotees.)

Iconography

Hindu iconography follows broad principles, not strict rules. Thus Lord Shiva has a blue skin almost all over India. However, in Kashmir and parts of Karnataka (to which people of Kashmiri origin had migrated) his skin is white. Hindu deities do not normally have facial or body hair, and yet Lord Shiva had a beard in nineteenth-century Bengal. Similarly, there is a temple in Rajasthan where Hanuman is shown as a wizened old man with a grey beard. Almost everywhere else he is youthful, muscular and beardless.

There is considerable diversity in the iconography of Hanuman. However, in most sculptures and paintings, he is shown with a human body, a monkey's face and a tail. The most common kind of Hanuman idol found in north India is a simple sculpture in relief, on a flat stone tablet. Hanuman faces right. He seems to be running from left to right, as if he is about to take off for his flight to Lanka. Sometimes the son of the wind is shown flying, again mostly from left to right. In both cases, his left arm is invariably raised upwards, the palm facing the sky and a hill resting on the palm. His right hand holds a club, which might either rest on the deity's shoulder or even be lifted above the shoulder. Saffron or vermillion paste is smeared all over the idol, not just on the portion raised in relief but also on the flat base. Such stone sculptures never had many details to begin with. The paste further obscures the little details that might exist. In paintings, the saffron or vermillion paste is absent and Hanuman's skin is yellow or golden.

In high art, Hanuman wears earrings made of an alloy of five metals. Tulasi Das wrote:

Your skin is like gold, and Your guise is fair
You have rings in Your ears, and matted hair.

There is, almost always, a helmet-shaped crown on Hanuman's head. Therefore, few artists bother about the hair. Similarly, very few icons show Hanuman holding a flag. Likewise, very few extant icons show him carrying a thunderbolt. Most artists consider it sufficient if he holds a mace, which is as strong as a thunderbolt. The bow is a weapon associated with Rama and not Hanuman. However, in some icons he wields one. A sacred thread—a janeu—worn diagonally across the chest would imply that Hanuman was a Brahmin. Most idols show him sporting this thread.

Like most male Hindu deities, Hanuman wears no garment on the chest. A fold of his loincloth is sometimes taken up diagonally across the chest and then diagonally down the back to the loincloth. In some elaborate idols found in Gujarat, Hanuman wears a regal, bejewelled cloak on the chest but his legs are bare. Deities like Rama and Krishna wear lower garments that cover their legs right down to the feet. They were kings and policy makers. Hanuman was a man constantly on the move. Therefore, his loincloth is normally shown wrapped around his thighs, leaving the lower legs bare. His loincloth, so to speak, is mostly girded up. It is made of the same material as the thunderbolt, we learn from the Oriya Mahabharata of Sharala Das and the Marathi *Bhavarth Ramayan*. It is as hard as adamantine and Hanuman was born wearing it. It is, thus, a male chastity belt.

On his feet Hanuman wears wooden sandals, in the tradition that his master, Rama, had followed while he was in exile. Such idols as have been sculpted in detail, and images that have been painted in the conventional figurative style, also depict Hanuman wearing several garlands and necklaces round his neck.

The second most popular depiction of Hanuman in art has him sitting or kneeling at the feet of Rama. In such representations, the Lord is always shown standing between his brother Lakshmana and wife Sita. Rama's brothers Bharata and Shatrughna often flank the three, in which case Rama and Sita might be shown sitting on thrones.

Another very popular pose that Hanuman is shown in is tearing his chest open with his bare hands. Rama, Sita, Lakshmana and, sometimes, Bharata and Shatrughna, are shown framed in the heart of the Supreme Devotee.

Because Hanuman spends almost all of his time either serving or worshipping Rama, he is often shown with folded hands and closed eyes, lost in thoughts of his master. In some parts of India, Hanuman is portrayed as a musician holding a veena.

On at least two occasions Hanuman had carried Rama and Lakshmana, together, on his shoulders. This is the subject of many paintings, especially in the Bhojpuri tradition as well as in calendar art. In most such paintings he is shown running (or flying) from right to left.

Many Hindu deities, especially some manifestations of the Mother Deity, are shown standing on the bleeding body of a demon whom they have lately slain. In some icons Hanuman, too, is shown doing this. The three best-known demons killed by Hanuman are Kalanemi, Mahi-Ravana and Ahi-Ravana. Any one of them could be the demon under Hanuman's feet. According to Devdutt Pattanaik, Hanuman is also sometimes depicted trampling a woman. This woman represents Panvati, baneful astrological influence, who represents unbridled lust as well. She might also be Ravana's sister Surpanakha.

Hanuman idols made of stone are the ones most commonly found. Metal idols, especially those made of gold, too, enjoy traditional sanction. Since the 1950s, idols made of plaster of Paris, ceramic, marble and other kitsch materials have become almost as common as the saffron-covered stone relief found in most villages.

A less-common form of Hanuman is the Panchmukhi—that which has five heads or faces. Each head represents an animal. The five animals are the monkey (male Vanaras normally dressed as monkeys), the horse (Haygriva), the lion (Narasimha), the boar (Varaha) and the eagle (Garuda). Some of these are incarnations of Lord Vishnu. There is also an eleven-headed (ekadashmukhi) Hanuman. These two forms are the result of the popularity of Tantrik cults during the medieval era. In such idols Hanuman has several pairs of arms. The five-headed Hanuman might have as many pairs of arms, or just one pair. The eleven-headed Hanuman normally has ten pairs of arms.

The postures in which deities are represented are called mudras in Sanskrit. Among Hanuman's best known mudras are the abhay (fearless or fear-removing) and varad (wish-granting or boon-giving) mudras. The two encapsulate all the qualities that have made Hanuman one of the most loved and accessible deities of the Hindu pantheon.

Immortality

Rama once said to Agastya, the saint, 'Ravana and Bali were great warriors. However, neither was a patch on Hanuman. Nor could they do incredible things of the kind that Hanuman could.'

Agastya replied, 'Hanuman was unaware of his own powers because of a curse. The many powers that the deities had given him when he was a child had made Hanuman a conceited person. He began to trouble the rishis. After a while this became unbearable. So, two rishis, called Bhrigu and Angiras, put a curse on Hanuman. They said, "We cannot take away your mighty powers. Therefore, we will cause you to forget that you have these powers. For a very long time may you be unaware of them." And that is what happened.

'During the conflict between Sugriva and Bali, Hanuman was in Sugriva's camp. But he was not able to use his great powers because he did not know that he possessed them.

'No one in the entire universe is as patient or intelligent, brave or wise, sober or sweet as Hanuman. His grammar is perfect and he knows all the great books of grammar: the sutrs, the vrittis, the Arth-pad and the Maha-bhashya. While he was learning grammar he would travel with Surya, the sun deity, from the Udaygiri mountain to the Ashtgiri. No one knows the Vedas like he does. He is a greater scholar than even Brihaspati. His powers are as mighty as the fire of doomsday.

'O Rama! God has created Hanuman, Sugriva and other great beings for you.'

Most of the Vanara nobles, including Sugriva and Hanuman, stayed on in Ayodhya for many months after the festivities of Rama's coronation were over. After a while Rama felt that it was not right to keep a king away from his kingdom for such a long period. So, he told Sugriva, 'Your people need you in Kishkindha. May peace and prosperity mark your reign.'

Hanuman said, 'Bless me, my Lord, and grant that I may always be loyal to you. I cannot bear to leave your company. But if songs about your divine virtues keep wafting into my ears, the pain of being away from you will get reduced somewhat.'

Rama rose and clutched Hanuman to his chest. He said, 'So be it. All your wishes will come true. You have helped me enormously. I will repay you with my own life. May you be protected from every trouble, from every danger.'

The king of Ayodhya then took off one of the necklaces that he had been wearing and put it around Hanuman's neck.

Many thousand years later the deity of death said to Rama, 'Lord Brahma has sent me here. He asked me to remind you that the deities await you in heaven.'

Rama replied, 'I will do as Lord Brahma wants me to.'

All the Vanaras, Bhalluks and rakshasas went to Ayodhya to bid farewell to Rama.

Rama granted immortality to Hanuman and Vibhishan. He told Vibhishan, 'You will not die as long as there is even a single human on this earth.'

Before returning to his divine home, the eighth incarnation of the Great Lord* said to his greatest devotee, 'And you, Hanuman, will live as long as the story of my life is told.'

---

* Valmiki writes that the deities informed Rama that he was the 'eighth Mahadev'. Other Hindu scholars consider him the seventh incarnation of Lord Vishnu.

Copyright Acknowledgements

Grateful acknowledgement is made to the following for permission to reprint copyright material from previously published Penguin books:

Bulbul Sharma for the excerpts from *The Book of Devi*, originally published 2001 (pages 129 to 238 in this book)

Namita Gokhale for the excerpts from *The Book of Shiva*, originally published 2001 (pages 19 to 35 in this book)

Nanditha Krishna for the excerpts from *The Book of Vishnu*, originally published 2001 (pages 37 to 127 and the section on Shri and Bhudevi from 175 to 176 in this book)

Parvez Dewan for the excerpts from *The Book of Hanuman*, originally published 2004 (pages 265 to 285 in this book)

Royina Grewal for the excerpts from *The Book of Ganesha*, originally published 2001 (pages 1 to 18 in this book)

Seema Mohanty for the excerpts and Devdutt Pattanaik for the illustration from *The Book of Kali*, originally published 2004 (pages 239 to 264 in this book)